EPPIE

EPPIE

The Story of Ann Landers

by
MARGO HOWARD

G. P. Putnam's Sons
New York

The author gratefully acknowledges permission from the following sources to
reprint material:
    Field Enterprises, Inc., for material from "Ann Landers," copyright
© 1959, 1965, 1967, 1969, 1974, 1975 by Field Enterprises, Inc.;
distributed by Field Newspaper Syndicate.
    Time Inc. for material from *Life* Magazine, copyright © 1958, Time Inc.
Reprinted with permission.

    All photographs in this book are from Margo Howard's personal collection,
except for the following:
    "Mother, Father and I": Chicago Photographers
    "Mother and Father during the happy years": Fred Schnell
    "With my husband Ken Howard": courtesy of Bonnie Colodzin

Library of Congress Cataloging in Publication Data

Howard, Margo, date.
    Eppie: The story of Ann Landers.

    1. Landers, Ann. 2. Journalist—United
States—Biography. I. Title.
PN4874.L23H68   1982   070'.92'4 [B]   82-3816
ISBN 0-399-12688-0   AACR2

Printed in the United States of America

Acknowledgments

My deep and sincere thanks to the aunts—Mickey Ferris, Dubbie Rubin, and Ruth Bean—for the lore which I had no way of knowing. To the DaSilvas, Albert and Gary, for expertise and encouragement. To Lynn Nesbit, for sticking around, and to Nora Ephron, for Lynn Nesbit. To Kathy Mitchell, for hunting up columns and correspondence. To Ellis Amburn, for guiding me through tricky waters. To my dear Ken, who gave me the benefit of his Amherst and Yale years, his artist's heart, and his love. And to my parents, who gave me a life better than any I could have dreamed up.

For Lercah, Beau, and Nute

Writers were not born to change the world.
We cannot even make it worse.
                    —Isaac Bashevis Singer

EPPIE

Chapter I

I picked him up on a train. I was twelve, Maybe my interest in this stranger came from a precocious instinct that here was a man of erudition and quality . . . and maybe the Statue of Liberty is in Lake Michigan. What actually got my attention was his nose.

It was a short, pushed-up snub nose, the kind that goads you into looking up its dark nose holes. Trying not to be rude, I'd make myself look away. But then I'd look back. I wondered how many times his friends had to see his nose before they didn't see his nose. It was a terrible fascination and I couldn't stop staring. To be truthful, his mouth was as riveting as his nose. It looked unfinished, as though he had started to melt. The lips were broad but not clearly defined. There was a gap between his two front teeth.

I couldn't see his eyes clearly, not even their color, because light was glinting off his glasses—thick lenses

13

banded in tortoise. And then there was his hair. It looked odd on a middle-aged man. The style was young but the color was old. If you didn't count his nose, the trademark of that face was the gray crew cut.

Our seats were in the club car. They were always in the club car. This was a train we rode a lot, Mother and I. The Four Hundred. It went from Minneapolis to Chicago with stops in between. We got on at in-between—Eau Claire, Wisconsin. We were frequent riders because Mother liked to go to Chicago. It wasn't that she didn't like Eau Claire, just that any town with a population of 32,000 would have made her a regular visitor to the nearest big city. When she went for a weekend, I usually got to go along. Father didn't always come with us because he was often elsewhere on business.

The things that made the club car special were the card tables and the bar. My routine was to overdose on ginger ale and play gin. I fancied myself a card-playing prodigy because I usually beat Mother, even though I could never remember what she discarded. It was not the last time I was to confuse luck with genius.

When our tournament was over on this particular trip, I chewed up some more time by twirling around in those big swivel armchairs which were screwed into the floor. I loved looking out the windows and watching the outside race by. The scenery was beautiful, even if I never knew what anything was. I didn't know, for example, the name of the river I had been looking at for years. Maybe I could ask the man with the nose. It was pointless to ask Mother: geography she didn't know from. We were to be in Nassau together, more than twenty years later, when she would ask me what body of water was outside our hotel. I said the

Mediterranean. That didn't sound right, she said, because that was the same water they had in Spain, which didn't seem terribly close at the time. I amended my answer: the Caribbean. We agreed that's what it was. It wasn't. The point is that geographic ignorance is hereditary in our family, and even at the age of twelve I was trying to reverse this genetic insufficiency . . . although I wasn't exactly sure how to go about it. Try asking a stranger? That might work. I would ask the man with the nose.

(I want to revise the remark about hereditary ignorance. I should have said that Mother's and my deficiencies were peculiar to the women in our family. Father was an ace at geography and had a sense of direction, to boot. He could also spell and we couldn't.)

I was certain of one thing, however. If I was going to ask my question, I'd better rehearse. I had spent so much time staring that I needed to make sure I didn't ask this person to please tell me the name of his nose. I practiced my question silently, then moved down one chair so that we were next to each other. "Excuse me," I said, leaning toward him, "do you know the name of that river?" Well, the man with the nose came through admirably. He didn't mind talking to a kid, and he knew the answer. It was the Baraboo River, and he was Wilbur C. Munnecke.

I had no idea what his appeal was, but I didn't want the conversation to end. I suspect, with hindsight, that the attraction was the same one which was to lure me again and again: I sensed his intelligence, and thought if I listened closely enough that I could be intelligent, too.

Because of the hour, I figured the best way to stay in league with this smart stranger was to invite him to dinner. He said that would be lovely and asked if I'd like to invite my mother. I said no. There followed a friendly discourse on the etiquette of traveling with companions, not to mention relatives. I invited my mother.

I truly loved the dining car. It was better than room service. Not only did the scenery have the good grace to change, but the waiters could do gymnastics and serve food at the same time. There wasn't a man among them who couldn't balance a tray perfectly as the train rounded a curve at eighty miles an hour. And they all called Mother "Mrs. Lederer," which somehow made it our train. (I was mystified years later when, planes having replaced trains, skycaps in different cities greeted Mother as "Mrs. Lederer." How did they know her name, I asked. They had all come from the Four Hundred.

What was an already perfect dinner—because it was on a train—was enhanced by the presence of someone new to talk to. Conversations where you introduced yourself were always more fun than when you knew who everybody was. My only regret was that my credentials were less distinguished than I would have liked, because I was a kid: I was a sixth-grader at the Campus School in Eau Claire and my teacher was Hazel Ramharter. My best friend was Sandra Caffee and I was an only child. Mother's credentials were better. She was a housewife who dabbled in Democratic politics.

Munnecke was married, he told us, to a woman named Sis. They lived in Chicago and had no children, but they had cats. He worked for Marshall Field IV, with the title of vice-president and business manager of Field Enterprises, Newspaper Division.

This was not just a train ride that yielded an odd-looking, smart-talking man. It was, rather, a wonderful refutation of the old maxim "Never talk to strangers," for by the time we got to Chicago, Wilbur C. Munnecke had metamorphosed into "Uncle Will" and we had made, the three of us, a dinner date for two weeks hence at the University Club of Chicago.

I remember none of the dinner conversation on the train beyond what I have told you. Unfortunately, when I was twelve—and even older—I had the self-absorbed habit of tuning out adult conversations unless they were about me. So not only do I not remember what was said, but also I feel certain I wasn't listening in the first place. Suffice it to say that *something* got said, because that train ride began a relationship between Munnecke and our family which was to deepen and endure. It would also change Mother's life, because three years later "Uncle Will" would make it possible for her to become Ann Landers.

Chapter 2

There was a national celebration the day Mother was born. It was the Fourth of July 1918. She was born with two front teeth and an identical twin sister. The names chosen for the baby girls were Esther Pauline and Pauline Esther, God forbid anybody should miss the point. When the twins arrived, they had two older sisters, Helen and Dorothy. A little boy had died in infancy. Their parents, Abe and Becky Friedman, were Russian Jewish immigrants who had settled in Sioux City, Iowa.

Fooling around with loose contractions of the babies' names, the family hit upon "Eppie" and "Popo." Mother was Eppie, the twin born first. She would later say, kidding on the square, that her seventeen and a half minutes' seniority made her wiser. Popo said it just made her older.

The Friedmans were busy with nicknames. Not only were Esther Pauline and Pauline Esther shortened to Eppie and Popo, but there were nicknames for the nicknames. Eppie was also "Eppela," and Popo was "Pesheh." Dorothy was "Dubby," and Helen was "Kenny." Later on, Mother even had a title attached to one of her nicknames: "Eppela with the *kepela*" (meaning "good head" in Yiddish). Mother said she got the name for being smart; Popo said she got it because it rhymed.

"The Friedman Twins," as they would be called for years, were adorable look-alikes with olive skin, coal-black hair, and spectacular blue eyes. As little girls, they wore their hair short, with bangs, giving them the look of two short extras in *The Mikado.* An enormous amount of attention came their way — not only because they were the youngest in the family but also because they were precocious, peppy, pretty . . . and two. They were always dressed alike and shared toys as well as friends.

Their mother passed on her feeling about the specialness of twins. "You love your sister best because you were each half an egg.:: Half a person? No one was to think about this until years later. Nobody knew from psychology then, at least no one named Friedman. The twinness, the alikeness, the togetherness, were always encouraged — and expected. The reward was attention.

The twins were never apart, even to spending most nights in the same bed. It wasn't that they each didn't *have* a bed, but it was harder to whisper if you weren't cuddling. They made things look kosher by putting a violin case in the empty bed. They had their secrets and they had each other. The world acknowledged them as a unit, and they grew into an odd little devoted couple. Sometimes there was even confusion about what had happened to whom. Their selfhood was blurry because their real identity came from being twins. Mother broke her arm when she was eleven; Popo thought it happened to her. They would tell each other's stories, and in their minds their lives became interchangeable.

Even their mischief was a joint venture, like the night they traveled around the house cutting off the fringe from the living-room rug and the lampshades. Then there was Mrs. Weiner's medicine cabinet. Mrs. Weiner lived across the street, such a pillar of the Jewish community that people called her *Mrs. Shul.* The twins were often invited over for milk and cookies. During one of these visits they excused themselves to go to the bathroom. The medicine cabinet caught their eye. Surely there was something they could *do* with it. And then it came to them: . . . they could empty the contents into the toilet, bottles and tubes included. After repeated flushing, the whole system was ruined and their father treated Mrs. Weiner to a new one. Of course the twins were punished. They were banished to their room. Together.

Being twins was not so much what Mother and Popo were as what they did. They were simply always together, thinking alike and operating as a pair of identical people. A pair of people, by the way, not unaware of the charm of two little girls who looked alike. And there were some who could never tell them apart. Such a hapless soul was their violin teacher. The twins would go for lessons after school. Popo was the better musician, so whenever Mother wasn't prepared, Popo would go in first, walk out when her lesson was over, and walk right back in to take another.

Although they were clinically identical, they did not look exactly alike. Mother was a little taller than Popo, and a bit more slender. She also had two dimples, and Popo had none. Their noses, as well, looked somewhat different; they were to look *more* different when Mother had hers fixed in her early twenties. Although claiming the Jewish girl's ailment—a deviated septum—she later conceded that she had never much liked her old nose in the first place.

Because they were raised with the example of parents who were always helping someone, the twins, too, wanted to do good. One mission of mercy occurred to them as they were walking downtown after violin lessons . . . two for Popo, none for Mother. Happening to look up at the barred windows of the county jail, it made perfect sense to them to walk into the building and ask to see the sheriff. Their offer? To play for the prisoners. They were ten years old.

And so they played their violins in the jail while a bemused sheriff stayed close by. The twins somehow decided it was their responsibility to make people feel good. They devised additional ways of cheering people up . . . such as visiting hospitals. They would get themselve in by pretending to be children of a patient. Kids under twelve weren't allowed in hospitals then, either, but the rule was not as strictly enforced as today. Of course they had no idea whom they were going to see; they just went from room to room and sang. It never occurred to them they might catch a terrible disease.

That the twins were outgoing was in no way unexpected. The four Friedman girls were, in different ways, performers. Helen, the eldest, started out to be an actress. She taught elocution while still in high school and at one time had thirty-two students. (A lesson cost fifty cents.) Instead of college, Helen attended the Goodman Theater School in Chicago, and then went on to do summer stock. Dorothy could see humor anywhere and was always "on." She understood the building of a joke and could transform the telling of an everyday event into a well-paced comedy routine.

The twins, of course, came to think that attention was their due, so they sang and danced at the slightest signal that someone might be interested. Put this together with Helen's piano playing and Dorothy's patter and imagine being in the same room with all of them at once. It is to understand the meaning of the word "headache."

The Depression hit when Mother was not yet a teenager. Like all children of that era, she was to carry into adulthood an understanding of doing without and making do, even though the Friedmans were in better shape than many families. The twins went to school with bag lunches that had extra everything to be shared with children who weren't bringing anything. They also took matters into their own hands about priorities. Given bus money every day for school, they would pocket the coins, walk the few miles, then appear at the ice-cream parlor at the end of the day.

The girls' sense of family was reinforced by close ties to other relatives living in Sioux City. There was a gang of cousins with whom they were particularly close, the Mirkins. Morrie Mirkin, a few years younger than the twins, was like a brother. He did, in fact, live in their house during his senior year in high school so he could more easily attend the "good" school, Central High.

By the time the twins got to high school, their sisters had married. Helen was Mrs. Dave Brodkey and moved to Omaha. Dorothy married Morey Rubin and stayed in Sioux City.

High school for the twins greatly resembled a coming-out party. They were quite social and rather well-known. Their father made them even better known by dolling them up in fur coats — the first and, I believe, only fur coats in the school. They were made of civet cat — a close cousin of skunk, to be sure — but fur nonetheless.

Carrying on the business of being twins, Mother and Popo would often appear at parties sharing one pocketbook and one escort. Theirs was a hard act to follow, let alone beat. The operative word, of course, was "act." Together they were a four-legged attention-getting device. What they did was overwhelm the boys and antagonize the girls.

If you get the idea that they were wonderful students, . . . close, but no cigar. Science and math did them in. Their geometry teacher, Mr. Littlejohn, served notice that they were in danger of having to repeat his course. Since they essentially took teachers, not subjects, they put their heads together, literally, and sang him an original ditty. It was to the tune of "Don't Blame Me," using close harmony.

> Don't blame me
> For flunking geometry
> I don't know a thing
> So that's why I'm singing
> Don't . . . blame . . . me.

They passed.

When the bookworms graduated from high school, they elected to attend Morningside College. It was a Methodist school and it was in Sioux City. The twins had no interest in going away.

College admissions in the mid-thirties were such that Mother remembers a recruiter from Wellesley showing up

24

and offering a place to any girl who could pay the freight and was not a certified moron. The Friedman twins, however, were not enticed by the siren song of an Eastern education. They were sticking with Morningside. Their devotion to a college education was subordinate to their interest in parties and traveling. Their own popularity and Papa's checkbook ensured numerous weekend invitations away from home. Even while in high school, the twins began going to fraternity weekends as the dates of Sioux City boys who were at the University of Minnesota. Of course they went together.

Another place they traveled to was California to join their parents during the winter. That they went for five or six weeks when their colleagues were attending college classes seems not to have been mentioned, at least by anyone from Morningside. In any case, during their Third Annual Self-Declared Winter Holiday Mother was introduced to a UCLA law student named Lewis Dreyer. He was from a family not unlike the Friedmans. The Dreyers were financially solid and Lewis' father was in the movie business. David Dreyer was a vice-president of RKO Pictures and a sometime collaborator of Irving Berlin's.

Lewis Dreyer proposed and Mother accepted. It was almost as though Popo had waited for Mother to find someone she wanted to marry, because the twins announced their engagement at the same time. Popo had had her fellow picked out for three years. He was Morton Phillips, the quiet son of an extremely wealthy family from Minneapolis. She had met him on a visit to the University of Minnesota when she was a senior in high school.

Well, talk about excitement! The "babies" would be married — in a double wedding, of course — to nice

25

Jewish boys from good families. The twins flashed their diamond rings and practived saying "Eppie Dreyer" and Popo Phillips." They also quit Morningside — surprise! They were going to be housewives, so what did it matter?

Chapter 3

The father of the brides was greatly enjoying the response to the twins' engagement. If Sioux City was expecting a knock-your-eyes-out, faint-and-die wedding, Abe Friedman was in a good position to deliver. He loved a party and had great pride-filled love for his youngest daughters. He also had the money and the friends. It was sister Helen, however, who took charge and really planned the wedding, for it was she who knew how these things were done. Abe and Becky did not feel socially surefooted enough to direct the printers, caterers, florists and musicians who would produce the extravaganza. The Friedmans wanted everything to be proper—to be American—and while they were certainly respected and substantial, they were also Russian immigrants.

They spoke English with a "broken handwriting," as Grandpa put it. Their main languages were Yiddish and

Russian, which the children picked up: the only problem being that they could never tell which words belonged to which language. Mother didn't know, until she was grown up, how much her parents' accented English affected her own speech. As a twenty-one-year-old bride she spoke of "door-to-door sa-less-men" and asked the butcher for "weal chops."

If the Friedmans were not quite comfortable with American ways, they knew very well what their own life was about. It was about family and it was about community. It was a given that you took care of each other, whether it was emotionally or financially. The twins, of course, were the ultimate in blood ties.

The Friedmans related differently to their children. A.B., as everyone called Abe Friedman, was warm and demonstrative. The twins could climb all over him, sit on his lap—one on each knee—and tousle his hair. Becky, however, was not outwardly affectionate and maintained physical distance, with only one exception. Dancing. She loved to play records on the Victrola and dance with her little girls. That became the symbol of warmth from their mother because it was her way of showing affection. To this day, the twins love to dance and spend hours on the dance floor at parties.

Becky had the same favorite song for quite a while, so the girls often found themselves dancing to a number that was not exactly in the top forty: "When Henry Ford Apologized to Me." It was done by a singer with a Yiddish accent and referred to the late Henry Ford's apology to the Jewish community. Ford Motor Company's anti-Semitism was so virulent that there was a boycott, making an apology a corporate necessity.

There were additional differences in approach besides one parent being huggy and the other not. A.B. was a source of encouragement to the girls. He let them know he thought they could do anything they set their minds to. Becky was more critical. Compliments did not exactly roll off her tongue. As teenagers, Mother and Popo would appear from their room all dressed up to go out. They would present themselves to their mother for approval. Her comment, more often than not, was, "You're going like *this?*" Sometimes she would elaborate. "How come Esther's dress is hanging in front and Pauline's is short in the back?"

Theirs was not a particularly bookish home. Rather, the emphasis was on success. And success to A.B. was simple: it meant doing well and doing good. Making money, and giving some of it away.

Abe Friedman knew from making money, or at least he learned. Fleeing conscription in the Czar's army, he arrived in America a young man with no skills, no education, no English, no nothing. What he did have were dreams and street smarts.

His first venture into the Americn free-enterprise system was peddling chickens from a pushcart. A.B. clearly understood cost control from the opening gun. He bought a one-eyed horse to pull the cart, the cheapest one available thanks to the defect. He reasoned that since you put blinders on the horse anyway, what was the difference?

A.B. did well enough on the street so that he could move indoors. He bought a little grocery store and said good-bye to the horse. His personality attracted customers and his kibitzing built a clientele. He was also casual about letting people buy on the cuff.

The "grawzery" flourished, but he was losing interest.

The kind of food A.B. wanted to sell was popcorn and candy. He wanted to sell the snacks that moviegoers ate . . . and while he was at it he thought he might as well own the theaters. He waited for his chance, and when it presented itself, he was ready. A theater came up for sale and he sold the little store. With two cronies, he bought his first theater in 1930, the World, a burlesque house. Next came the Hippodrome, which everyone called the Hip. Talkies were still new and A.B. was betting against Harry Warner, of Warner brothers, who was skeptical about talking pictures. Warner's famous question in those days was, "Who the hell wants to hear an actor talk?"

Mr. A.B., as his new employees called him, had finally found his dream career. It was a fortuitous coming together of his love for people and his love of pizzazz. He was, instinctively, at home in the movie business. He told people, whenever it came up, that he was in "the show business."

Eventually he became a partner in a tristate chain of theaters. By the time Mother was in her teens, Abe Friedman was one of the successful citizens of Sioux City. He also had "investments"—an insurance agency; the distributorship for Miller's beer; apartment houses; ice factories; and Friedman's Department Store in Le Mars, Iowa, in partnership with his brother, Gail—but it was "the show business" he mentioned when asked what he did.

I was not above mentioning it, myself, as a little girl. When my cousins and I would visit Sioux City, it was our great joy to zip past the ticket takers with the magical phrase "Mr. Friedman's grandchildren"—and, of course, no tickets. The Orpheum Theater was my favorite, having the longest candy counter and the nicest manager's office, where, privileged people that we were, we could leave our coats and use the phone.

I remember A.B. from those years as a sweet-faced man with dimples, wire-rim bifocals, and silvery temples. He usually had a Florida tan and, I thought, great twinkle. He was a meticulous dresser who always appeared in public with silk tie and handkerchief, diamond stickpin, and an even bigger diamond ring. I loved to play with the sparkling stones and made several youthful, unrewarded attempts to get him to give them to me. If he looked a touch flashy, perhaps that was his way of not being poor anymore. It was also his great pleasure to buy jewelry for Becky, whom many people spoke of as a great beauty with flawless skin. A stylish, ahead-of-her-time lady, Becky designed many of her own clothes. Her passion was high heels, probably because she was barely five-foot-three. The four girls, all a smidgen shorter than she, were given high heels about a minute and a half after their fourteenth birthdays. Black patent pumps were favored. Along with jars of Vaseline to shine the shoes, those pumps were the Friedman girls' welcome to womanhood. Mother called them her Minnie Mouse shoes.

Theirs was a household of women, and A.B. loved it. Becky's priority was that everything be just the way Papa wanted it. She catered to him from morning till night, and as he grew more prosperous, morning began at noon.

By today's standards, she ran a tight ship. The girls regarded her as the ballast, the strong one. Her word was law, and the children did not skate by without responsibilities. They all had their jobs, and they did them.

Becky was sickly, on and off, and there were periods

when she coped by not coping. Helen, seven years older than the twins and two years older than Dorothy, became the matriarchal figure who took responsibility for the younger ones. For her pains, she earned the name of "the bossy one."

Becky's social life was more proscribed than A.B.'s, both because of her personality and the times. Her main outside interest was the gathering of "the ladies" for a standing poker game. Becky didn't drink anything alcoholic, but whenever she played cards she always smoked a few cigarettes. Mother guessed that was her way of being fashionable.

If Grandma insulated herself to some degree, A.B.'s turf was the state of Iowa. He knew everybody, and everybody ranged from civic leaders to hookers, politicians to shop-keepers. He was warm and outgoing and loved to be "between people." He flourished on social interaction . . . and it didn't hurt business any, either.

A.B. had a number of Gentile friends, which was a source of pride for him. When he would tell stories of gatherings he had attended, the prelude was always the same: "Arthur Sanford and I were the only Jews there." He was proud of his entrée into non-Jewish circles because assimilation had not really happened yet and anti-Semitism was quite pointed, quite often. One of his close friends was Guy Gillette, the senator from Iowa. Whenever A.B. returned home after having been Gillette's guest, the girls knew the report would begin: "Arthur Sanford and I were the only Jews there."

There was another place where he was surely the only Jew: St. Joseph's Home for Unwed Mothers. "For some mysterious reason," Mother once remarked, "Papa felt very close to Catholics and was always doing something for

Catholic charities." His favorite was St. Joseph's and he often visited with their mother superior. After one of their chats he decided what the girls needed most was entertainment. In those days, they didn't leave the establishment to roam around and entertain themselves. It was presumed they had already done that. So who better to arrange a diversion for them than someone in "the show business." A.B. began sending a projectionist to St. Joe's on Sundays to run movies for the girls.

Becky, as well, had a high compassion quotient. More to the point, she was a famous soft touch. If anyone rang her bell in need, he was not turned away. During the lean years, starting in the late twenties, the bums would chalk an X on the sidewalk outside any house where they could get a meal. The Friedmans of course had an X. What they should've had was the seal of the Innkeepers of America, for in addition to feeding people, Becky always had to make sure they had a place to sleep. Her generosity usually meant there was a "guest" in the basement. Never mindthat four girls lived in the house—nobody thought about that then.

The Gentlemen of the Basement did lawn chores—if they were up to it—in exchange for room and board. The best-remembered chap was Conway. Everyone marveled at his sunny disposition, never a sad expresion or a complaint. Only when he departed Villa Friedman was the source of his happiness discovered. Conway had tapped into a barrel of Passover wine, helped himself to several jugs of vinegar, and was, in fact, schnockered every waking minute.

In addition to the bums in the basement, there were often dinner guests who found it convenient to stay the night. This group was mostly from "the show business," prizefighters and vaudevillians who had not yet achieved

33

fame or the price of a hotel room. They would roll in and out of Sioux City to play Grandpa's theaters, then move on to the next town.

Grandma's favorite was a fighter named Buzz—"Bawz," she called him. He was always welcome at Becky's. The girls knew, without being told, when he was coming for dinner. There would be a little extra effort, a little something special. Suppressing a smile, heir mother would announce just before dinner, "Bawz is back."

Like her husband, Becky could be wonderfully funny. Sometimes her humor had an edge to it, other times it was simply unintentional, like a Gracie Allen routine. There was the trip she took with A.B. to Chicago to buy lamps. Their first stop was at Marshall Field's, where the lamp department was famously large. As soon as they stepped off the elevator, Becky glanced over at the rows and rows of lamps. Without taking one step into the department she shook her head and sighed, "You know what? Nothing catches mine eye." They left.

Her touch was light. Mother loved a telephone conversation that took place over and over when she and Popo were young. They would call home after school to find out what was for dinner. The answer was always the same. "You'll be here, you'll see." Then the girls would ask, "Well, what are you doing?"

"I'm dancing."

"Are you alone?"

"No. I've got an orchestra."

Everyone in the family shared a sense of humor. It was their entertainment as well as their way of being strong. Laughter was a good defense against what life could dream up to do to you. If you could laugh, then you might not cry. And if you pulled off the humor well enough, the reward was attention and approval.

A.B. was prone to making homilies, although they were often funny because his English was a little mixed-up. He would instruct one and all: Cast your bread on the waters and you will get back sandwiches." He was an easygoing philosopher who seemed to know why things were the way they were. Perhaps it was the experience of fleeing, surviving, and then prevailing which gave Abe Friedman his philosophical bent. Mother called him the Jewish Lin Yutang. She has mentioned that one observation of his, in particular, comes back to her over and over. It is that "Nobody ever calls you up to give you something."

A.B. was certainly in a position to have learned this firsthand. His acquaintance with hardship, and then his success, made him a logical source of help for those in need. He became used to people calling him up to ask for things, and depending on the situation he would give a gift, make a loan, or find a job. Some good works were even disguised as poker games.

From the time he had serious money, A.B. was part of a high-stakes poker game. When they played at the Friedmans', any child who happened by the front room could hear A.B. designate a side pot for someone who needed assistance. "This one's for Mrs. Goldstein. We'll buy her coal." "This pot's for Nate. The doctor says he's not ready to go back to work yet."

The poker games, of course—both Becky's and A.B.'s— became forums for discussing the twins' wedding. Everyone had suggestions for what they all agreed would be an

35

Event. Close friends already knew they could look forward to twin brides, three rabbis, twenty-six attendants, seven hundred guests, and a wedding such as Sioux City had never seen.

Chapter 4

With light hearts and Papa's charge accounts, the twins began shopping for trousseaux. Whizzing from one floor to another at T. S. Martin's, the brides-to-be tried on whatever caught their fancy. Suits were in. The new look was shorter, narrower skirts with bolero jackets. As always, they bought everything alike.

Clothes shopping was fun, but there was plenty of time for that. The real business of the day was selecting wedding veils. When the twins walked into the millinery department, the buyer himself took care of them—probably because Esther Mirkin worked there and had been raving about her adorable twin cousins. The buyer was a young man who had come from a store in Lansing, Michigan. He was twenty-one, a few months older than the twins. He was also blond and handsome. Quite taken with Mother, he was most attentive and just kept on talking. He wasn't sure he could get anywhere, though. It was perfectly clear that these girls were not cruising around buying wedding veils on speculation.

While Mother was seated at a little table looking in a mirror at the seed-pearl-and-satin possibilities, the young buyer took Popo aside. Did she think there was a chance, he asked, that her sister might go with him to a Hadassah dance? Popo said to try. "All she can say is no."

The youthful milliner gave it a shot. To her own surprise, Mother accepted. He had made the sale. His name was Jules Lederer.

The twins left the store and talked excitedly about Mother's impulsive decision. They both knew it was half a beat off to be engaged to one man and accept a date with another. On the other hand, if she was attracted to this new person, then maybe she shouldn't be engaged. Things were sounding rather crazy. Not only had this stranger sold them wedding veils, but Mother had agreed to go to a dance with him. And all she really knew was that he was charming and had a beautiful face.

After the dance, she knew more. She knew she wasn't going to marry Lewis Dreyer. The twins endlessly talked it through. Would their folks be disappointed? Would Lewis be all right? And how would it look, since they had set the date and the whole thing had been announced in the Sioux City papers? A.B. answered one of their questions. Upon learning of the new development, he was sympathetic and supportive. Driving Mother to the post office to mail back the ring, he offered the comfort that not a few fathers before him had given: "Better now than later."

What would happen to all the plans for a double wedding? Nothing. In a matter of a few weeks, after one of the shorter courtships on record, Mother decided there would simply be a substitution of a groom. She would marry Jules Lederer, who had been very quick to ask. Of course, by the time all this got figured out, Mother knew more about her young man than when she accepted that first date. She knew he was from a large family in Detroit and that no one had much money—him included. He never finished high school and had worked full-time from the age of sixteen.

Comparisons may be odious, but several people made them anyway. Mother's decision certainly took her out of the ranks of clever girls. She was turning down a beau in law school who came from a rich family for someone with no education, to speak of, who sent some of each paycheck home to his mother. The move bespoke daring to some, *mishagias* to others, but the decision was made. The only formality remaining was for Lederer to pass muster with Becky and A.B. The Friedmans had met him, of course, but now they planned a special evening so they could get to know him and ask him questions—like "Are you Jewish?" He was, and said so, although the blondness and the finely chiseled nose said maybe not. "Say something in Yiddish," A.B. suggested.

A small problem. Both Lederer's parents spoke some Yiddish, but he had made himself unaware of it. He was either not paying attention or didn't care to learn. To please A.B., he did the best he could. "I vanna take a valk." Miraculously, the conversation continued. In truth, A.B. was charmed. Remembering his own beginnings with the chickens and the pushcart, he decided that the twenty-one-year-old millinery buyer had "potential," that he was a comer and a scrapper with a future. Also, any young man with the nerve to try to pawn off "I vanna take a valk" as Yiddish was all right in his book.

Becky, too, gave her approval . . . a high compliment, given the situation. Not exactly a mother's dream, this high-school dropout with no visible assets. But the young man *was* charming, and clearly crazy about Eppie. Having made up her mind, Becky set about putting the young suitor at ease. Resting her chin in two bejeweled hands, she smiled and said, 'Ve are very simple people."

Father's ties to home and family were not nearly as strong as Mother's. He had a quality of autonomy, of aloneness, that struck her as both foreign and appealing. His family did, however, surpass the Friedmans in one regard. There were simply more of them.

Father was born November 15, 1917, in Detroit—the third of seven children. He had two older sisters, three younger, and one brother. (His eldest sister, Irene, was my sentimental favorite because she married two men named Sullivan. Her Jewish mother, alas, didn't think it was so cute.)

Father beat the rap of being a middle child by becoming first among equals. He was the favorite. His brother and sisters always knew that he was *the* kid to their parents. Not only was he a wonderful child to look at, winning and bright, but also he was indulged and fussed over. He was also the repository of his father's hopes. Morris Lederer's pet name for him even made this clear. Boemel. It meant "tree" in Yiddish and signified ht the beautiful, blond, smart son was the root source of his father's dreams. The other kids referred to him, somewhat less deferentially, as

40

Kid *Gefarelach,* which meant "terrible." His mother always called him Sonny.

Despite Father's election as favorite, all the children had great confidence. No doubt it came from Grandma Gustie, who was quite a snob about her offspring. By her lights they were more intelligent than other people's children, more adorable, and just generally terrific. Her hopes for their achievements were unbounded and her ambitions for them no secret. It didn't matter to her that he was a Romanian immigrant with no education;the children had a model for success, and it was their father, Morris. He had come to Detroit as a little boy from England. With dogged drive, natural gifts, and no help from anyone, he had earned a reputation as a great salesman—traveling variety. Hs wares were ladies' aprons and small notions, which he sold to stores throughout the Midwest. He wasn't home all that much, but Gustie understood that he was doing what he loved. She also had a wonderful antidote for loneliness. Seven kids.

Morris was able to sock away enough money to open a factory which manufactured housedresses. His biggest customer was the S. S. Kresge chain. He couldn't kick the habit of being on the road, however, so he decided to take in a partner to run the business while he sold. He sent for his younger brother, Jack, to come from New York. Life was comfortable and the business grew. There was money enough for the Jewish family of Catholic proportions. Gustie, in celebration, wrote checks . . . although with no particular understanding of how the money got in on the other end.

She was not without a sense of humor, and certainly not

without an instinct for drama. Gustie never had just an ordinary cold, it was always the worst, most agonizing, head-swelling, energy-robbing cold of anyone in the world. If the four-foot-ten mother of seven was a bit of a hypochondriac with the purpose of keeping her children concerned, it worked.

To the chagrin of the Detroit public-school system, Morris took Boemel on the road with him quite often. It was on these trips that they grew close and the son learned the father's selling techniques. Before he was a teenager the young Jules had made many a call with his father and got to see what salesmanship was all about. His childhood was really quite simple: it was that of the adored son. He hung out with his old man whenever he could and was doted on by a house full of women.

Childhood ended abruptly. Morris' car hit a train at a crossing in Jackson, Michigan. He was dead at forty-nine. Gustie was thirty-seven, Father was thirteen. His beloved role model/hero-teacher/father-chum was gone, and with him the family's financial well-being. Grandma was left a modest trust fund, but she continued to write checks at the same rate as when her husband was alive. Because of procedures she didn't understand, she no longer had an interest in the factory. The young widow with seven children soon ran out of funds. The family would be, for a time, on public assistance.

All the children who were old enough went to work. A barely teenage Jules delivered papers before school (sometimes with the help of his older sister, Ruthie, who had been persuaded that it was an "honor" to be allowed to help). He also sold Christmas cards and wreaths in season, shoveled walks in winter, and took whatever part-time jobs he could get.

There seemed to be no particular feeling of poverty. With or without both parents, a lot of kids were scrambling. The Depression was taking its toll. Not having enough to eat was no big deal; the real deprivation the young boy felt was the loss of the person he loved best, and never knowing what might have been.

The family's need and his own impatience convinced the teenage boy to quit school in the eleventh grade. He went to work full-time and his formal education was finished. The sixteen-year-old head of his family became a stock boy at Kern's Department Store in Detroit, where he also ran the freight elevator and unwrapped ladies' hats. Someone in the millinery department spotted him as a bright, aggressive youngster and took him under his wing. Jules decided that retail selling was for him . . . except that it probably wasn't a decision at all; more likely it was his father's conversations stored up in his head, as well as the blood in his veins. The goal, of course, was to become rich; to carry out Morris' dreams, to take away Gustie's hardships, and to achieve the ease and standing he associated with money. The idea was to win.

By the time he was seventeen, the stockroom was a long-ago training ground and his position was assistant manager for millinery at Herpolsheimer's Department Store in Grand Rapids. Home was the Y and take-home pay was eighteen dollars a week, six of which was sent to Gustie. At nineteen he was accomplished enough to become manager of ladies' millinery at the J. W. Knapp Co. in Lansing.

Then came another promotion, to T. S. Martin's in Sioux City.

It was a lucky accident, or maybe no accident at all, that Jules Lederer should find himself selling hats to women. He was one of those guys who could sell anything to women. Often, what they really wanted was him. People thought he looked like Kirk Douglas and they responded to his earnest, boyish charm. The manner and the looks made him a natural as a ladies' man. Struggling, yes. Lonesome, no.

Gustie was distressed that "Sonny's" preference was for *shiksas*. She spent a lot of time wishing that he should please find a nice Jewish girl. He found one in Sioux City.

It was part of his salesmanship that he could get people to pay attention to him. Mother certainly did, that afternoon in the millinery department. "You're the first girl I ever met," he told her, "that I wanted to marry . . . and you're coming in to buy a wedding veil." Who could say no to that? Who did?

Chapter 5

On July 2, 1939, the twins walked down the aisle of Shaare-Zion Synagogue. They were twenty-one. As always, they went together. A.B. had a bride on each arm. The brunette belles wore identical gowns of heavy slipper satin. The twins had chosen that material because it was their idea of the perfect bride's dress. Unfortunately, the day was everyone's idea of summer in Ethiopia. It was 103 in the shade.

If the sisters had given new meaning to the concept of radiant heat, they also looked exactly as they had planned: dramatic. The fatefully romantic wedding veils floated down from Russian-style coronets. The satin-and-seed-pearl headpieces looked very Catherine the Great. Each twin wore a single strand of pearls and carried a heart-shaped satin muff covered with purple-throated white orchids.

Looking somewhat cooler were the bridesmaids, all

eleven of them, dressed in rainbow pastels. Their wide-brimmed hats to match gave them the look of a garden-party staged by Ziegfeld. Nosegays of deep red roses offset the pale frocks, and each girl wore a five-strand pearl choker. There was, of course, a groomsman escorting each bridesmaid, so there were twenty-two attendants, two grooms, two brides, and one father participating in the ceremony. Also three rabbis, the Friedmans having decided to cover all bases with the inclusion of Orthodox, Conservative, and Reformed clergymen.

The ceremony was a piece of dazzle. It was sumptuous, grand, and sentimental. It also resembled the mob scene from *Quo Vadis.* There were 750 guests, not including a few hundred more people who showed up just to stand outside and watch. Mounted police were on hand to keep order. With spotlights, it would have been a premiere. The whole affair was, in fact, recorded on film. Not that home movies were common in those days, but the father of the brides was, remember, in "the show business."

A.B.'s gift of friendship was never more apparent than on this day. All his buddies were there, from poker, politics, business, and the theaters. Of course Popo's new in-laws came from Minneapolis, and a small Lederer delegation from Detroit. Mother had met them only the day before.

The cast of hundreds moved downtown to the ballroom of the Martin Hotel. First, there was a reception, then a dinner for three hundred. For those few hours it was hard to remember that great numbers of people were out of work, that a five-cent hot dog with chili was a luxury for many, and FDR was predicting war. For that little bit of time, the reception line superseded the bread line. The occasion was one of memories and new beginnings. The "babies" had left the nest and Becky danced the night away to "Moonglow," "Stardust," "It Had to Be You." Glenn Miller tunes were everybody's favorites . . . maybe because he was from Iowa.

The newlyweds took the night train to Chicago. The twins, of course, were going on their honeymoon together. You thought maybe marriage would make them want to be apart?

When they arrived in Chicago, the foursome went to the Edgewater Beach Hotel, a sprawling pink affair on the shores of Lake Michigan. The desk clerk asked for proof that the baby-faced couples were married. Having been forewarned about the ways of the big city, the girls produced "proof" from inside their hatboxes.

No question about it, the "babies" were married. Their enormous double wedding not only testified to the legality of the unions but also symbolized the togetherness of the twins who had been raised as one. The joint ceremony was a statement that the sisters were still a unit. The subtler statement, however, was that they had — for the first time — made different choices. One twin had chosen a reserved, rich college boy. The other had thrown in her lot with a guy who had raised himself on the streets, didn't have a dime, and looked like *goyim* into the bargain. For whatever reason, Mother had decided to gamble. Maybe it was her first unconscious effort to be different. Maybe it was a stab at not being twins anymore.

That their lives were no longer exactly alike was pointed up in less than a week. After fewer days than he had figured, Father ran out of money. Cutting their honeymoon short, the Lederers returned to Sioux City to begin married life. The Phillipses continued on to Banff and Lake Louise. It was the first time that Mother and Popo had ever been apart.

Back in Sioux City, Father returned to work as the newly married head of a household. Mother tried to figure out what a household was. As the youngest in the family, she and Popo had not been paying terribly close attention.

The newly minted Mrs. Lederer made typical brides' blunders . . . like boiling the lambchops. The dear girl had misheard the instructions. But she persevered and asked a lot of questions. Within weeks, she learned about groceries, laundry, ironing, and bills. She also learned something else. They were expecting.

Father made the customary late-night runs for ice cream and they discussed the future over butter brickle and pickles. The two of them made all kinds of plans, one of which was to name the baby Mark. They somehow knew it would be a boy.

I was born on March 15, 1940. They went to work finding a new name. Their garde was not avant enough to stick with "Mark." First things first, however. Soon after the delivery, Mother requested ice cream and then called Popo in Minneapolis to tell her the news.

Over butter brickle—no pickles—the rookie parents chose the name Margo. The daughter of friends had that name and they liked the child. They were bound to use an M, for in the Jewish tradition of honoring the dead I was to be named for Morris Lederer. Symbolically it was a perfect choice; before the age of six months, I was already traveling.

48

We lived in eight cities by the time I was seven. A vagabond would have been jealous. The roster was Sioux City, St. Louis, back to Sioux City, New Orleans, Milwaukee, Los Angeles, Chicago, then Eau Claire. Father would be offered a better job, and off they'd go. A better job meant ten dollars more a week. Mother always moved to the next place with a sense of adventure. She thought women who balked at leaving family and friends were silly. It was her belief, often stated, that "you go where the grapes grow." I therefore assumed, as a preschooler, that Father sold not only hats but also fresh fruit.

My parents' recollections of those scrambling years were bathed in the amber light of fond memories. Nothing seemed tough, it just seemed like fun. Mother would marvel, later on, that as a young housewife she could make dinner using seven cents' worth of perch. It was a matter of pride that even having been raised rich, she could manage on whatever there was. With no splurging, Father's paycheck could cover their needs. And when they lived in Sioux City, of course, movies were free.

Chapter 6

The first place I remember is New Orleans. I had already turned two. We lived in a little house on St. Charles Avenue and Father ran the millinery department at Marx-Isaacs. Mother was the Mah-Jongg queen, and I spent hours making pictures with the tiles.

Since there was a war going on, decency demanded that one not spend all one's time playing Mah-Jongg, so Mother did her part by joining the American Women's Volunteer Service. She was kind of a military candy-striper at La Garde Naval Hospital . . . .shades of singing for the patients. She even took me sometimes, to sing and dance for the soldiers.

It was at La Garde were Mother met a dermatologist who headed one of the units. He was tall and gawky and smart. It was the smart part that interested her.

The doctor's name was Robert Stolar. Although Mother

knew he wasn't Jewish, she invited him home for a Passover dinner. It seemed like a nice occasion to entertain a guest. The good doctor showed up two hours late. His hostess was furious. Had he never heard of a telephone? Well . . . he needed to see "a few more patients." And while they were speaking of telephones, Stolar asked if he might call his mother in Washington. His end of the conversation took place entirely in Yiddish. Mother was amazed. She hadn't figured the doctor with the ill-fitting clothes and the slow way of speaking for Jewish.

God forbid a guest in her home shouldn't see her pride and joy, Mother brought Stolar into my room and woke me up to meet him. I was thrilled to be included. To show my pleasure, I jumped up and down in the crib and pulled down my pants. Appalled at the exhibition, Mother berated me with a "naughty-naughty, bad-bad."

When I had been put back to bed, Stolar told Mother—in front of Father—that her response to my action was quite odd, considering that I was only three. They talked some, and Mother mentioned that I stuttered noticeably and had asthma. He gingerly said something along the lines of, "Well, of course she does! You're making her crazy."

What Stolar had to say wasn't very flattering, but she listened. It was as though some part of her understood, without thinking about it, that here was someone who knew what he was talking about.

Mother and "the derm," as Father called him, began a friendship. It would become a teacher-student relationship—not unlike Pygmalion-Galatea. Stolar would come to be Mother's de facto psychiatrist—not that she thought she needed one—but she had so many questions and it felt good to have someone to talk to. If she never intended to see a psyhiatrist, the relationship worked out fine, because he wasn't one. What he was was understanding and wise, and willing to give her his time.

He would be around from then on. The habitually tardy, brilliant bachelor doctor became the Answer Man. His and Mother's friendship would undergo some changes, but it would last. In time he would serve, though with less intensity, as informal shrink/adviser to both Father and me. He was unique, Stolar, and he filled an unusual place in our lives. He would become immersed in our family's problems and often serve as the arbiter. For years I coudn't decide how I felt about this man who had such intimate knowledge of us all. I didn't know if he was a once-in-a-lifetime friend, a Svengali, or a usurper of my father's decision-making powers. I hated him, I lied to him, I loved him, and as I write, I know that he has been a steadying force in my life.

A true scholar, Stolar used to read in bed as a little boy after he was supposedly asleep. I have heard from others that he is one of a limited number of people with an IQ of 200. He became a dermatologist because that was the field that offered the best scholarship. He became an expert on leprosy and found a treatment for the skin disease vitiligo. And it was he who understood pigmentation so well that he finally was able to make black skin white. Without taking psychiatric boards, Stolar became well-acquainted with the field because he discovered that so many skin problems were generated by emotions.

Perhaps with genius goes peculiarity, which I thought he had in abundance. His speech was exceedingly slow and deliberate, with just the vaguest hint of a Southern accent. He would also not answer a question in fifty words if he could answer it in five hundred. As I grew older, I sometimes wouldn't know what the hell he was talking about. And then, always a few days later, I understood what had been said. He was vague and fey and I have never met anyone remotely like him. He was to marry but never have children. It occurred to me that maybe *I* was his children.

In any case, that first unpunctual dinner was followed by others. Number one on "Uncle Bob's" agenda was my asthma. Convinced it was psychogenic, he set out to cure it . . . and he did. It took him ten years.

The second thing he addressed himself to may have been said to be Popo. After listening to Mother talk, he knew that she was too busy being a twin. The flow of phone calls, letters, and visits between the sisters was constant. I wound up a little bit stuck in the middle of all this. The twins were still thick as thieves, but my presence made a difference. Because Mother had a child, her emotional connection to Popo was diffused. The result was that the aunt who looked like my mother was competitive with me for her—and I returned the compliment. Our difficulties, even when I was a little girl, were veiled, but they were there. Not that we each didn't have a trump card. Popo had an alter ego; I had asthma. Her own first child was born when I was two, but by then the pattern had been set.

Mother, of course, was off in Disneyland on this subject and had no idea that there was any friction. She thought Stolar was nuts to even suggest such a thing . . . after all, she loved her sister best because they were each half an egg.

Never did a psychiatrist—even an unofficial one—have such fertile ground to work. Neither Mother nor Popo had ever acknowledged that there were competitive feelings built into the twin business. They were emotionally joined at the hip and years of training had made them disavow any uncomfortable feelings connected with being twins.

Stolar went to work to get Mother to begin to extricate herself from the debilitiating aspects of twinship. It would take years of talking. As he strove to negate Mother's deep sense of what Aristotle called "a single soul dwelling in two bodies," he would also map out strategies by which she could forge an identity of her own. His plan was for her to become somebody.

Chapter 7

Father was drafted in 1944. He went to war in Arkansas. His assignment was to Camp Robinson in Little Rock. Fate, apparently, was wearing an Uncle Sam suit, because another soldier stationed there was to become his dearest friend and determine the direction of his life. It was his brother-in-law Morton Phillips, whom he knew only slightly. That the twins' husbands would wind up together for basic training was an odd coincidence, to be sure. That their time in the Army would cement a profound friendship was an even stranger twist. Jules Lederer and Morton Phillips would form an alliance which was to last for thirty years.

My only recollection of this time is of one night in Sioux City. Mother had returned home to live with her parents when Father was drafted. On the night I remember, there was eerie activity in the Friedman house. Becky had been brought home, ill, from a poker game. No one knew what was the matter, but Mother was with her in the living room when she lost consciousness. Their last conversation was Mother telling her, "You're going to be all right," and Becky answering faintly, in Yiddish, "I hope so, little one." Then she was gone, dead at fifty-six of a cerebral hemorrhage.

Father and Morton got emergency leave for the funeral. Not long after, they were mustered out. It was 1945. Father had to decide what to do about going back to work. The millinery business would have been an automatic, except for the fact that Morton offered him a job. One of the Phillips-owned companies was Guardian Service, a line of cookware sold door-to-door. Father was offered a job with Guardian in Los Angeles, and accepted. He couldn't know how far the millinery business would take him if he went back to it, just as he couldn't know what future there would be in accepting Morton's offer. Instinct made up his mind, and perhaps a desire to be more officially connected to Morton.

The only thing I remember about Los Angeles was that my room was not exactly my room. I slept on a cot in the kitchen. Mother made her way in yet another new town, and Father hit the street.

The distinguishing feature of Guardian Service was that it was waterless cookware designed to retain vitamins. The spiel went something like this: "Good morning, madam. Are you interested in your family's health? Of course you are. And do you know that when you boil vegetables, all the precious vitamins and minerals go down the drain with the water?" Father was then in the lady's kitchen making sad faces about her old-fashioned pots and pans. While she was still feeling guilty about robbing her family of vitamins and minerals, Father made his pitch. If she would invite four other couples to dinner, he and his assistant would put on a demonstration dinner; they would bring the food, prepare it, serve, and leave the kitchen spotless. The only thing Father asked in return was the chance to deliver a chalk talk about the benefits of waterless cooking. Once this was done, he would take orders — often selling a complete set of Guardian to every couple present. I can still see those pots. They looked like aluminum with goose bumps and had thick clear glass covers.

The system was to work neighborhoods, many of which were ethnic. As a result, Father picked up a little Polish and a lot of Spanish. When his assistant was unable to make it — an event that occurred with remarkable regularity — Mother would fill in. She would do the cutting and peeling, help serve, and then do the dishes. Although it was rather mindless work, it offered a break in the routine of looking after a small child, and it was an undeniable help to Father. They spoke of this time, years later, with great affection and warmth.

Father sold his pots and pans seven days and seven nights a week. He didn't bother with days off because nothing was more fun than setting the world on fire. He was doing wonderfully, and once again he was selling to women . . . or maybe he was doing wonderfully *because* he was selling to women. It seemed hard for people to say no to this slender, handsome, boyish young man. Within six months he had broken the company's national sales record, having put on more dinners and sold more pots than any other salesman in the organization. He was promoted to district sales manager in Chicago. The grapes were growing in the Midwest again.

Chicago was a great improvement as far as I was concerned, if only in terms of sleeping arrangements. This time *I* had the bedroom and my folks used the Murphy bed in the living room. Our apartment was on Chicago's South Side in a modest building called the Saranac. I was in first grade at Bret Harte School, where I made the first friends I can remember: Franny Rosenbacher and Linda Goldstein. Linda was the only one who had a television then, which clearly made her a wonderful friend to have.

Mother's energy was propelling her to do something with her time, only she didn't know what to do. The drive was there, but no direction. It was during this period that she began encouraging me to eat Planter's Peanuts. She didn't make me, exactly, but there was a bit of the feeling of a forced march. Planter's Peanuts, you see, ran jingle contests, and a label was required with each entry. Mother was taking no chances: when she sent in one entry, she would immediately go to work on another. Her rhyming abilities were quite good, actually. She wrote funny poems to friends and called them "Eppiegrams." Popo, too, sent verses to chums, signing hers "Edgar Allan Popo."

There was a card table in the living room that served as Mother's jingle office. It had rhyming dictionaries, piles of paper, pencils, and of course those wretched peanuts. I don't remember that she ever won anything major — maybe little prizes, but certainly no cars or trips.

Father's contest was with himself. He would roll in around midnight, usually with a trainee, to hash over the dinner they had just put on. His other salesmen knew that if they were in the neighborhood they were welcome, too.

The coffee was always on and Mother was the burger chef. After six months in Chicago, Father's district led the country and racked up new records. Morris Lederer's son, the salesman, was promoted to the parent company, the one that made pressure cookers. This time the moving van went to Eau Claire, Wisconsin. Father's title would be vice-president in charge of sales.

National Presto Industries was a family business, and the family was Morton's. His father, Jay Phillips, was chairman of the board, his uncle Louie was president, and he himself was executive vice-president. Aside from a fleeting thought about all those relatives, Mother and Father viewed the job as a wonderful opportunity. Not only would Jules Lederer become a corporate VP in the appliance big leagues, but Morton and "Julie" could resume their Army friendship. Father's advancement to the decision-making suites of Presto more than outweighed the fact that he would be working for his brother-in-law. As for the twins, they were thrilled — they would be living in the same town again, at last.

Chapter 8

Eau Claire had 32,000 people, the presto factory, and U.S. Rubber. Of course there were shopkeepers and doctors and some of everybody else, but the two factories were essentially what Eau Claire was about.

Our first house was a tiny white frame at 1617 Valmont Avenue. It had a small square front yeard and a long narrow one in back. There were two bedrooms and one bath. Popo named it "Peanut Place."

I was enrolled in second grade at the Campus School, an extension of the University of Wisconsin. being part of a teachers college, we had practice teachers marching in and out. There were one-way glass partitions in the classrooms so the student teachers could observe and not be seen. I may have gone all through elementary school playing to an unseen audience. An audience I could see was made available soon after I started second grade. The college drama department asked for two little people to play Medea's children. I was one. For five nights I and my "brother" put on short white togas and got to lie onstage. Dead. That was my first encounter with The Theater.

I was a devoted student and got mostly A's. There were comments sent home from time to time that I was a bit chatty when other people were talking and not so good at following directions, but other than that everything was fine. My real interest was art and I became insane with making posters. No effort was too great. When our class did a unit on Alaska, I was downtown begging ermine tails from the furrier. When we did Hawaii, I glued up dozens of macadamia nuts in the shape of an orchid. I was clearly crazy.

To lead an idyllic small-town life, I thought, you had to have a dog. No one of the parental persuasion was looking for a pet, but they agreed to give it a try. I wanted a boxer. We found a breeder and bought a puppy: Lady Presto. She was a truly stupid animal, but I thought she was wonderful. Of course none of us knew from training a dog, so we muddled along with a rolled-up newspaper and our most authoritative rendition of the word "no."

Lady Presto would greet Father by standing up with her paws on his shoulder and threatening to lick him to death. We waved the newspaper and said "No." It didn't work. After several months with an ill-trained animal who closely resembled a pony, it was decided (not by me, I might add) that Lady Presto should be given to a farmer so she could roam around freely.

The best pets, though, were at Popo's. She had monkeys. The twins had always been mad for monkeys. They even made monkey faces. Mother would sometimes make an "aper" at me, in public, as a loving secret signal . . . except that it was usually so far from secret that I would pretend not to see. In any case, Popo's monkeys were a gift from a South American friend of Morton's who learned of the affinity. They were small and cute and she named them david and Bathsheba. They lived in a cage in her backyard when they weren't busy escaping. The fire department was called more than once to snatch them from neighbors' trees. When this wore thin, the darling couple became a contribution to the zoo.

The years in Eau Claire meant a great deal of traffic from our house to Popo's. She lived in a big two-story corner house with a split-level backyard. I got to know my cousins Etta Jean and Edward. Jeannie was two years younger than I, and Wardo three years younger than she. They had a governess, Edith Strasberger. Strassie was tough, Germanic, and very proper. Popo also usually employed a couple—one of which wasn't really a couple, a fact she asked that they conceal from the children.

The Phillipses lived differently from us. They had three in help; we had Mrs. Sather once a week. Their house was spacious and rather formal; ours was four rooms, with the biggest space being the basement. Their kids didn't often eat dinner with them—which struck me as wonderful! Spending so much time with grown-ups, I thought it was a real treat not to have to listen to adult discourse.

I used to love to go to Popo's, preferably when she wasn't home. There were so many things to do over there. Her shoes, for one thing, would keep Jeannie and me busy for hours. Popo was the only one of the sisters to retain her fondness for high heels, and all her shoes had platforms. Jeannie and I would try on pair after pair and put on shoe shows. We made Edward be the audience. There was also a record player in Popo's bedroom with records that the kids didn't have. To hell with Mother Goose set to music. In Popo's room we could listen to Pearl Bailey and Dorothy Shay, "The Park Avenue Hillbilly."

If there was a lot to do at Popo's, there was also a lot to eat. She was a wonderful baker and her desserts had more than a casual acquaintance with chocolate and whipped cream. I remember one confection, in particuar. I saw it in the center of her refrigerator one day after school. It was a gorgeous three-layer cake covered with whipped cream, shredded coconut, and shaved chocolate. I don't know what got into me, but I got into it. The problem was that I did it with my hand. Popo discovered the mess, formerly known as dessert—for company, yet—and icily called me Hogmouth. The name hung on for years.

There was, as always, continual friction between Popo and me. There was nothing out of this world going on, just sniping at each other whenever a chance presented itself. I would occasionally overhear my parents regretting that she would "get down to" my "level."

Popo and I found odd little arenas for our difficulties. It was as though I would dream up some bit of behavior to which she could respond with either unkindness or under-standing. She seldom went with the friendlier choice. I remember the night we and the Phillipses were sitting on folding chairs in a rented hall. We had come to hear Jeannie play in a piano recital. I was seated next to Popo. My attention landed on her big new heart-shaped diamond ring. They didn't call her Sparkle Plenty for nothing. I whispered, pointed, and feigned a swoon so she would let me try it on. To get rid of me, she handed it over. I put it on and admired it . . . my hand always moving to catch the light. I did this through "Babbling Brook," "Clair de Lune," and three Mozart pieces.

Hogmouth had apparently metamorphosed into Big Knuckles, because Popo signaled for me to return the ring and I couldn't get if off. She was furious and hissed at me to try harder. I whimpered that during the intermission I would go to the ladies' room and use soap to loosen it. She said something about the fire department, and all I could think of was that they would use a blowtorch. Then Popo would have her ring and I would have nine fingers. Fear got the ring moving, and I handed it back.

Our troubles were seldom more serious than that. Our relationship was not all-out warfare and it was not fraught with unpleasantness all the time. It was more like being nibbled to death by ducks. The situation was not helped by the fact that there were comparisons between the twins' daughters. Both mothers were not above pointing out the deficiencies of the other's child. My imperfections must have been the more numerous because Popo had the most to say.

Jeannie and I, miraculously, were friends and did many things together. I was the elder, so of course there was a bit of worship going on, which I thought made for a very fine friendship. One of our joint activities was Sunday school. Mother decided it was time for me to learn about my "heritage." She couldn't, unfortunately, have picked a worse town for heritage-learning. There were thirty Jewish families in Eau Claire, and naturally no temple. What there was was the Knights of Columbus Hall, which was rented every Sunday morning by interested Jewish families. The students, obviously, were all ages, so graded classes were a problem. The more important problem, however, was that no one in town was qualified to teach, and the enterprise had been limping along with an imported rabbinical student from Minneapolis. The deal was for every Sunday, but it worked out to be nowhere near every Sunday. The severe winters and reliance on the bus made it more like one Sunday in three. The result was that I didn't learn a whole lot, heritage-wise. To this day Mother wonders why I am not more religious.

The understanding when Father went with Presto was that he would travel one-third of the time. It turned out to be half. He was never so happy. Traveling gve him a feeling of well-being and importance. He was totally at home on the road, as his father had been. Gypsy blood, the two of them.

Father adored the appliance business. He seemed to the pressure cooker born. I tried, therefore, to be circumspect about my fear of that enormous pot filled with fifteen pounds of pressure—even though it did make wonderful corn on the cob. I was not circumspect enough, apparently for father got wind of my phobia and arranged cooking lessons at the plant. Their home economist, Dorothy, had the good fortune of teaching a preadolescent the tricks of the trade. I showed up one day a week after school, and soon was making all sorts of exotic things . . . like jelly. The hitch was that I could cook only in a pressure cooker, which meant that I could cook only with Dorothy. I would have no more used that thing on my own than I wuld have roller-skated to Kenosha.

If Presto made it possible for me to learn to cook—sort of—it taught Mother to be alone. The traveling that father loved made a different kind of life from what she had known before Eau Claire. One way she adjusted was to zero in on me. We seemed to be talking all the time. I was encouraged, no doubt with the guidance of Dr. Spock, to "express myself." I got the hang of it so well that I don't think I had a thought I didn't share with her. She, in turn, began to drill into me all her values and perceptions. I had no idea what I was listening to half the time.

One thing I heard a lot about was Principles. I got so sick of hearing about Principles that I would shriek my worst insult: "You're so . . . principalic!"

Mother's biggest wish, I think, was that I know everything there was to know. She often used to tell me, "If I could only put my brains in your head." Alas, she couldn't, and I was stuck with my own.

Chapter 9

The gospel, according to only children, is that you are never hard up for attention. Something about single-offspring status invites a weird combination of watchfulness and adoration.

In exchange for all the attention coming my way it seemed the least I could do was be interesting, and my idea of interesting was to talk all the time. Mother recorded in my baby book that I never shut up, stuttered a mile a minute, and had a knock out vocabulary. At two and a half she noted my use of the words "preposterous" and "caduceus." Since I do not now know the meaning of "caduceus," I suspect I may have been coached.

My playing habits were also recorded. Forty years ago Mother had these observations:

Most toys leave her cold. Margo prefers a powder puff to most anything. Rita Stonehill got her an educational toy—a knockout bench. She knocked herself out with the mallet. Ruthie Bean got her a little tea set in Detroit. She pours water in the cups and spills it on the rug.

Margo would rather play with my hats and Daddy's ties than toys. Ray Schear bought her an invisible blackboard. It soon became invisible. Her dad bought her a wicker doll carriage. In three days the bolts, nuts and screws were missing. Daddy also bought her a dollhouse from New York (Macy's). It had paper furniture. She sat on the chairs and sofas. We find her very destructive.

That entry is inexplicably follwed by this one: "Margo is beautifully trained." Then the notations become less flattering. "Margo ignores older women but loves men and boys." The comment that suggests mild dementia is the one that says I used to do the rumba at odd times—there didn't even have to be music. Just as other children would break into song for no apparent reason, so I would break into a rumba.

From the age of three and a half, my favorite way to play dress up was with a friend. That way we could be "Eppie" and "Popo." If I thought it was intriguing that there were, in a way, two of my mother, she found it appealing that I would go through life alone. With me, she could see what it must be like to be a single child, set apart, sharing nothing.

The pattern that I spend a lot of time wih adults was established early. My fourth birthday was celebrated by going to the floor show at the Blue Room. For better or worse, I was one of those kids said to be six going on eighteen. It was no surprise that my conversation was precocious.

The irony was that while my mouth had free rein, the rest of me did not. I was never allowed to have a bike and was always driven to school. Mother was protective and to some extent fearful, so my activities were restricted. The reason I couldn't have a bike was that she had seen a child knocked off one by a car. She never told me that, of course; Bob Stolar did, years later. (Although I don't remember her stated explanation at the time, it was probably something along the lines of repeated pedaling being bad for lower-leg circulation.) I understood, eventually, that a cautious mother was an occupational hazard of being an only child.

I was not allowed to take the bus to school in Eau Claire. Mother said she was up in the morning anyway, and it was no trouble. What was trouble, apparently, was to get dressed; her driving outfit was always a coat over a nightgown. In the winter, particularly, she was a vision— floor-length nightie, fuzzy slippers, and a knee-length mink coat. There was never anyone but me to appreciate her get up . . . until the morning she was stopped for speeding. Then a whole bunch of people could admire it, because she was instructed to go to the police station. She didn't have to go there because she had been issued a ticket, but because she couldn't prove who she was. A driver's license was not in her nightgown.

Once at the station, Mother went straight to Bernie Garmeier's office. He was the chief of police. In Eau Claire it was no big deal to know such officials by their first names, so Mother laid into "Bernie" about how the arresting officer must have been gunning for her because she wasn't going any faster than anyone else. She seemed to feel strongly about it —and who, after all, wanted a scene with a lady in a nightgown?—so "Bernie"suggested they forget the whole thing. Mother thought that was equitable.

I was sent to camp at the age of seven. Although no one told me then—or ever—how this decision had been reached, I had a strong hunch that Dr. Stolar had recommended it. The choice was Camp Louise, two hours outside Washington, D.C., where he lived. He was the medical director and spent his weekends there.

There were two sessions, five weeks each. I was "allowed" to go for the full ten weeks. This is interesting only because I didn't want to go at all. Furious, I showed my displeasure by getting a killer attack of asthma on the plane to Washington.

The logistics of that first summer were repeated for the next seven years. Bob would meet us at the airport—never on time— and Mother and I would spend the night as the Statler. The next day Bob and his new wife, Frances, would drive us to camp. Mother would stay the weekend, then leave with the Stolars.

Camp Louise was enormous. There were 350 campers and a huge staff. It was known as a dramatic camp, with many of its theater and dance councelors coming from Juilliard. Bubbles Silverman (Beverly Sills) was probably the most famous camper, who discovered her life's work in those summer productions. For me it was a wonderful chance to pursue my interest in "the show business." The summer I played the little boy in *The King and I*, one of the producers from the Broadway *King and I* was in the audience. He got word to Mother that I was as good as the kid they had in New York—and was she interested in my doing anything? She was not. Theater was the last thing she had in mind for me. It made perfect sense to her, however, to put me in a camp where the emphasis was on the performing arts. She hadn't chosen the place, after all, for its theater activities . . . she had picked it because Stolar was there on weekends.

This was no stage mother, at least in the sense of wanting me to be on the stage. She had aspirations for her only child, but acting wasn't one of them. She was certainly nothing like Darryl and Dwayne Hickman's mother, whom Darryl confronted when he was in his thirties: "Why did you take me to the studios when I was three and start with those goddamn movies?" "Because," she answered sweetly, "it's what you always wanted to do."

One of the highlights of each camp season was a ten-mile hike to Camp Airy, our brother camp. I always wanted to go but Mother worried about my asthma and never gave permission. I must have seemed pathetic being turned down, year after year, so Stolar and the camp honchos figured out a way for me to go. I found out halfway through the hike that "Uncle Airy's" limousine was following on a nearby road, just in case "someone" had an asthma attack. Someone didn't.

The last summer I spent at camp I was thirteen. As usual, I got off the plane wheezing like a broken-down motor and breathing with great difficulty. Stolar met us— miraculously on time—and told Mother to go on to the hotel, that he would handle things. Then he put me in his car and the two of us drove off. I was sure we were going to his office for a shot of Adrenalin in peanut oil. "We are going sightseeing," he announced. We were going *where?* I could barely breathe. He told me the time had come to say good-bye to asthma. I told him I would prefer Adrenalin in peanut oil.

I lost. We went sightseeing, and the sight was the Washington Monument. As a favor, he drawled, we would only have to walk up. We could take the elevator down. Then I knew he was crazy.

Stolar said there were "about 300" steps. There were 898. He talked to me the whole time, saying things I had heard him say before. The conversation—one sided, to be sure—was about responding to problems, my mother, anger, and frustration. The gist of it was that I had to learn to leave my breathing apparatus out of things and start coping more intellectually. I would have to make myself stop acting out the childish insult "You make me sick!"

By the time we had walked all the way up and stepped into the elevator, my breathing was normal and the asthma was gone forever. Stolar had known for ten years, ever since he met me, that the illness was psychosomatic . . . and he had proven it with that lousy walk up a million steps.

It was during that last summer at camp that A.B. died of cancer. All four sisters had spent the previous winter spelling each other at the Mayo Clinic, where he was being treated. Mother thought he was sixty-three, although nobody could be sure. Few immigrants of that generation had records.

She phoned to tell me the news. I spent the whole day crying in the cabin. The sadness didn't come from the loss of someone I was close to, for I didn't know A.B. that well.

The sorrow came with the realization that people could die, and that Mother felt so bereft. Her Jewish Lin Yutang was gone, and she would speak of him, from then on, with great idealized love. Mother believed she had been his favorite child.

Chapter 10

If energy were diamonds, Mother would have been De Beers. During the first decade of her marriage she had a restess drive and not the faintest idea what to do with it. Her dilemma was the vocational version of "all dressed up and no place to go."

With an only child in school all day and a husband who traveled three or four days a week, it was unlikely that her attentions could be turned homeward. Working women were unusual then in her circle, so a job never seemed like a possibility. Women whose husbands made a good living were more inclined to "find" themselves in Bonwit's or at the bridge table. Alas, Mother didn't play cards, and the Mah-Jongg set had long ago been put away.

Stolar provided an answer, or at least a start. He pointed her down the volunteer route. The key was to get involved, be busy. Mother responded by becoming a Gray Lady at the hospital, a member of the League of Women Voters, a reader for the blind. She joined a few civic charities for good measure, and in no time at all she hadn't a minute to spare.

She was the busiest mother in town . . . and an ecumenical one, at that. Like her father, she was drawn to Catholics. I would often come home from school to find either Father Paul or Father Brady. Father Paul was noteworthy because he was so handsome, Father Brady because of his cigars. He might as well have been smoking a rope. Mother and the Fathers were always planning one thing or another. She would help them figure out fund-raising affairs, offer advice about public-relations problems, and just generally see to it that interfaith matters didn't get balled up. Oh, yes, and she was a board member of the National Council of Christians and Jews, too.

A little later on she would connect with Bishop Fulton Sheen and take Catholic instruction from him. Not only did she wish to learn about the Church, but she had it in mind to get something taken out of Catholic-school textbooks: she didn't like the part about the Jews killing Christ. She was lobbying around with Sheen for years about this, and although that part was finally deleted, it is doubtful that Bishop Sheen did the deleting.

I remember a trip to New York when we saw him. He called for us at our hotel in his limousine. Presumably he belonged to an order that cared only about chastity and obedience. He was wearing a spectacular wristwatch. It was shaped like a cross and made of heavy gold.

Another time he called the hotel in New York when Mother was out. We chatted a bit and he asked me to tell her he would come by at six o'clock. I wrote the following note: "The pope called. He's coming at six." Mother told note: "The pope called. He's coming at six." Mother told him of my clerical error and said he was amused. What made him less hppy, however, was finding out that Mother had no plans to convert.

If Eau Claire was small, it at least allowed Mother to learn the ropes of charities and women's groups. She was drawn into the community and learned to become part of a larger world. She became an avid newspaper reader. It was the best way she knew to keep track of what was going on. The paper was the Eau Claire *Leader & Telegram*. Its owner-editor was a prematurely white-haired, red-nosed, hard-drinking newsman named Marshall Atkinson. He called Mother Sunshine. Her name for him was Moonshine. Whenever there was a civic fight going on, Marshall Atkinson knew he could count on Eppie for fiery give-'em-hell letters to the editor.

In the early fifties Mother wound up at a meeting of local Democrates, certainly not a chic place to be. In a state of La Follette liberals, Eau Claire was a Republican bastion. She went with her girlfriend Blondie Brigham, and one meeting was all she needed. The texture of local politics appealed to her, and the ragtag nature of the Democratic orgainzation offered a challenge. Good-bye to the ladies' groups. Mother's mission became clear: she would see to it that there was Good Government.

In her quest to see that the Democrats flourished, she was a rookie with people such as Gaylord Nelson, Bill Proxmire, and Henry Reuss. Her new heroine was Eleanor Roosevelt. After learning the ropes in a crash-course kind of way, Mother decided it was necessary to commit herself to her fellow-citizen activists. She announced she was running for county chairman of the Democratic party. Her opponent was certainly interesting: he was head of the union at Presto.

As far as Eau Claire was concerned, the contest was one of mythic proportions. The cocktail parties hadn't been so lively since the son of a lumber millionaire ran off with one of the girls in Woolworth's. In overstated and simplistic terms, the election was between the workingman/union leader and the dilettante/executive's wife. (Footnote: Father was a good sport about it. He didn't tell her not to. What he did do was become state chairman of Citizens for Ike, about as clear a statement as he could think of that he did not share his wife's Democratic leanings.)

Mother was a candidate. She showed up at coffees and meetings looking for votes. It was a hotly contested battle, with the opposition dubbing her "the society wife of a Presto bigwig."

When the votes were tallied, she had lost . . . .only, she didn't think she had. Going to Matt Atkinson, she made a statement which was the next day's headline: "ELECTION RIGGED, STACKED, AND PACKED . . . .A PHONY." Certain there had been Chicago-style fooling with the ballots, Mother demanded a recount. Some of her own supporters called her foolish. Then they called her Madam Chairman. She had won.

Politics filled both days and nights. She would harness her naivete, her big mouth, her charm, and her guts to take her to the top of state politics. This meant, of course, a whole new circle of friends. Father's absences didn't seem so painful anymore, and whether she knew it or not, this was the first time that there was no Popo with whom to share the spotlight. The sister act was retired, at least for the time being.

82

If toiling in the Democratic vineyeards was work, you couldn't prove it by Mother. She was thrilled with the tumult, and there was hardly enough time for the phone calls, lists, and meetings. One of the first matters which demanded her attention was whom to slate for a congressional seat. The candidate she and her advisers came up with was a farmer, Clement Zablocki. They chose him not because he was perfect but because he was willing. (Not only did he run and win, he is still there currently serving as chairman of the House Foreign Affairs Committee.)

Stolar encouraged her to make the most of her new situation, to get to know people who were, as he put it, "operating at a good level." Mother gave it a try. On her next trip to Washington she went to the visitors' gallery in the Senate to hear the country's business being transacted. The young Hubert Humphrey was making a speech. He would certainly be someone worth knowing, she figured, so she sent down a note asking to meet him. The Minnesota senator looked up to the gallery and saw the pretty brunette with the dimples. he nodded and gestured that she should come down and meet him off the Senate floor when he was through speaking. He was true to form. She waited quite a while.

The two neighboring-state Democrats had a lot to talk about. They started a friendship which would last until Hubert died. He became a close family friend and opened the doors of Washington to Mother. A party, a meeting, an introduction, would lead to new friends on the Hill. What she wanted was to learn, and the way she learned was to listen to people who knew what she wanted to know. Listening was followed by a volley of questions. It sure beat reading.

Margo Howard

Mother, even then, was fearless and outspoken. She was also funny and had it in her to be tough as nails. When Alexander Wiley was the senior senator from Wisconsin, Mother encountered him in a receiving line at the White House. Wiley stopped everything by telling her, in great detail, about his most recent ailment. She thought he was going on overly long in response to the question "How are you?" When he finally reported that he may have contracted a bug, Mother patted his hand, smiled, and said, "Nothing trivial, I hope," then moved down the line. She had proved to herself that it doesn't matter what you say in such situations, because nobody's listening anyway.

Wisconsin's other senator at that time was Joe McCarthy. Not only did she believe he had a screw loose but also she had seen some of his mayhem firsthand. A few close friends of hers and Father's had been let go from university and industrial positions because McCarthy's soft-on-Communism diatribes had frightened all but the morally sturdy. She knew it wasn't much, but whenever she found herself in his presence, she refused to shake hands or engage in conversation.

Mother did more than symbolically show her disdain by refusing to speak or shake hands. The last time McCarthy ran for the Senate, she devoted months to mobilizing her organization to beat him. There was extra adrenalin in her efforts, and extra hours. She even went back to ringing doorbells and fund-raising, something she hadn't done since her days as a beginner earning the right to run for county chairman.

McCarthy won that race, but it was his smallest margin ever, 100,000 votes. Mother blamed herself for having missed the last two weeks of the campaign. She had taken a

84

vacation with Father and imagined that those 100,000 votes had been from people whose doorbells she hadn't rung. As far as she was concerned, McCarthy's last victory had been her first failure. Nobody agreed with her, of course, but her sense of her own power convinced her that if she had pulled out all the stops she could have made it.

Chapter 11

Traveling, for Father, was an instinct, like a diabetic's craving for sugar. For Mother it was an acquired taste. Moving around became a leitmotif of their relationship, something they could do together. He made changing the scene a part of her life. It had been a mutual choice, after all, to live in one city, then another, and to take trips just for the fun of it. If there were times when Mother would have preferred to stay home, she never said so. Their time together was prized, and even her commitment to politics came second.

Although Mother joked that there were two ways to travel — first-class and with children — I was almost always with them when they left town together. Our ratio seemed different from other families', all the kids I knew took trips with their parents only once in a while, but for me, staying home was unusual.

A trip we made over and over was to Chicago. We took the Four Hundred and stayed at the Ambassador East. Part of every trip was spent in the hotel beauty salon. Mother made me go with her. I would sit on two phone books while someone did my hair. Mother thought it would be fun for me. She also thought it would be nice if I had a special rinse of lemon juice and peroxide. Father thought I was blond until I was in my teens.

The best part of going to the beauty shop was being invited into the back room, where a friend of the shopowner made hats. The young milliner from Indiana was always gracious about letting me play with the flowers and ribbons he used for decoration. His name was Halston.

One resident manager at the Ambassador who survived my childhood was Eliot Miselle, an Australian. It was he who introduced me to movie stars in the lobby and let me go in the office to look up people's credit ratings. He also taught me some Aussy slang which turned out to be rather earthy. *Fiar dinkum bludger,* I think it was. Father was amused, Mother was not. She was unbending about off-color language. If I wanted to repeat something involving a verboten word (I knew only two), I had to do it by referring to "the S. word" or "the F. word." Stolar thought we was way off base. Words were just words, he told her, and shouldn't be glamorized by prohibition. He could never make any headway on the subject.

I was not the only one who couldn't cross Mother's verbal boundaries. She wouldn't listen to "the S. word" or "the F. word" from her peers, either. If unlaundered language crept into the conversation, she would call the speaker on it. Most people felt chastised and embarrassed, as if they had thoughtlessly called Queen Elizabeth "honey." A few people, however, felt no remorse. One woman informed her that she had been in polite society for a long time and didn't need lessons about what was all right to say.

Chicago, at least for Mother and me, was a weekend place. The longer trips were to warmer climates. They were the best chance the three of us had to be together. In Eau Claire, Father was preoccupied, working late, or gone. The winter vacations meant that we could hang out together and do nothing in particular. With every trip, Father vowed he would put business out of his mind and recharge his batteries. A day or two into these trips, however, he invariable struck up a conversation with another man who was resting up from corporate responsibilities. Then the two of them would talk business.

We went on these extended holidays from the time we moved to Eau Claire. So did Father's collection of papers, graphs, and charts, "in case the weather was bad." Doing nothing made him restless, so he worked wherever he was. When I went to the beach with a floating mattress, he would be there too . . . with marketing studies. If I wanted to hang around the pool, he would come with me, all the while writing down ideas in his Recorday notebook, which he was never without. His business, for me, was symbolized by the five or six briefcases and the Dictaphone he took everywhere. Father was a workaholic, although I don't think the word had much currency then. Mother accepted (or tolerated) his single-mindedness because there was no way to change it. It was part of who he was and perhaps what had attracted her in the first place.

Popo and Morton hung out in Palm Springs in the winter, so one year we went there, too. Just as Mother gravitated to political figures, Popo's enthusiasm was for movie people. She even had a little part once, in Dean Martin and Jerry Lewis' film *At War with the Army*.

We took a bungelow at the Biltmore, where I rode horses with a wrangler, walked Joan Crawford's dog, did homework that had been sent with me, and took my yearly, doomed-to-failure swimming lessons. Mother couldn't swim either, so I assumed everybody just took the lessons and got no results.

Mother's daytime agenda was to sunbathe by the pool. She didn't give it up until years later when Stolar finally convinced her that if she didn't cut it out her skin would look like a relief map of Pakistan. Until she kicked the habit, though, her routine was to lie flat, like an immobile oil slick. When the young woman in the chaise next to her noticed one morning that they shared the same coloring, she suggested that Mother throw away her tanning oil and switch to Jergen's lotion. There weren't many women she would take poolside advice from, considering herself something of a beauty maven, but this time was different: the adviser was Elizabeth Taylor. The beautiful young star and Mother got into a conversation and then looked for each other every day after that so they could visit in the sun.

Taylor was genuinely friendly and sweet, the penalty for her goodness being that she couldn't get rid of me. I was asking questions, bringing her towels, fetching ice water — anything I could think of. The only thing I didn't think of was that she might not be looking for a preadolescent friend. She was then about twenty, a great beauty whose eyes really were lavender. She liked comic books and so did I. The only difference was that her mother hadn't forbidden her to read them, so she shared hers with me.

One morning, hearing Mother wonder out loud what to do with me because there was a party that night, Taylor offered to baby-sit. She said she had a script to read and that looking after me wouldn't be any trouble. Never did I imagine life could be so wonderful.

Taylor and her then beau, Stanley Donen, spent the evening with me. In my mind the three of us were best friends. After that, whenever we saw "Elizabeth and Stanley" at dinner, I was insane with worship. If Mother was trying to dampen my interest in performers and in "the show business," Palm Springs was not the place to be.

There was one other trip that made an impression. We sailed to Hawaii on the *Lurline*. The first night at dinner Father looked around the dining room and fixated on a small older man sitting several tables away. He became agitated and beckoned the captain. Would he please give that man over there his card? We watched as it was done; Father didn't say a word. The man for whom it was intended took the card, looked visibly ill, then left the dining room. I was spellbound watching this happen, and Mother had no idea what it all meant. The explanation was that the man was from Detroit and had been the lawyer for Father's uncle—the uncle who had been in business with his father. There was family lore which some of Morris Lederer's children believed, and others didn't, that their uncle's lawyer had done something with the will (disposed of it, to be exact), thereby cheating their mother of her interest in the factory. Father was one of the believers.

Once we docked and settled into the Royal Hawaiian, Mother dealt with the suitcases and Father invited me downstairs for a look around. As we walked across the lobby, there was the man from the boat. What followed was a scene that showed a side of my father I had never seen before. He walked up to the older man, raised him off the floor by his collar, and spoke words that had me wide-eyed. "I should kill you for what you did to my mother." Like a wave receding, Father's fury dissipated. He put the man down, took me by the hand, and walked into the bar. He never discussed the incident with me then or ever.

By the next day the terrible and strange spectacle of Father's anger moved out of my thoughts. I had work to do. This was the winter of the suntan pills. I had never once gotten tan. Stolar said the reason was that I had no melanin in my skin, the pigment which permits darkening. I always felt gypped going back to school looking as though I had gone nowhere, so I had been pestering Stolar to figure something out. He said if I would faithfully time myself in the sun, he would give me pills to make me tan. The caveat, however, was that if I overdid, I would be *very sorry*. (The pills were meant for blacks who had vitiligo, the splotchy skin disease.)

During part of the allotted time, I would cover my face, except for my nose and the tops of my cheeks. Mother saw this one day and asked what I was doing. I told her I was making freckles. "You have perfect skin," she snapped, angrier than I had seen her in a long time. "Normal people try to get *rid* of freckles." This was turning into some trip. First Father tells some man he'd like to kill him, then Mother makes it plain she feels like killing me. There seemed to be no way I could make her understand that the idea of perfect never appealed to me. I also wanted braces and glasses, and I didn't need my hair lightened. The signals I was getting were mixed. If my values and behavior were what really mattered, why was it so important what I looked like? Mother was not clear about this herself. We played out one scene, over and over, that crystallized my dilemma. Mother would select my clothes carefully, polish my shoes, brush and arrange my long blond curls, and put a dab of rouge on my mouth. Then, when someone would remark on what a beautiful child I was, Mother would demur and respond, "Oh, we don't care about that. What matters is that she's a nice girl." Oh, really? What I finally figured out was that good looks were important but you should deny them, or at least pretend they didn't count.

This war between doing one thing and saying another was Mother's struggle with things as they were and things as they should be. Her goal, in any event, was to perfect her presentational self and also the product of that self: her child.

Chapter 12

My parents were not what you'd call sporty. Mother was totally nonatheletic, probably because her mother believed that ladies didn't do that sort of thing, and father was always too busy—or thought he was. Exercise for him was reaching for the phone. For Mother it was turning the pages of *The Progressive*. Their only stab at organized sport was to take up golf at the Eau Claire Country Club. A friend talked them into it. Soon they both established handicaps. Their swings. After two months, Mother's clubs were stolen, which she took as a sign from God that she wasn't supposed to play. Father interpreted the omen to include him, too, so that was that.

The absence of diversions does not necessarily indicate seriousness; sometimes it merely indicates the absence of diversions. Father's interest in business was undiluted and wholehearted. When he wasn't actually working, he was talking about it, usually to Mother. I heard much of what was said and somehow made the erroneous connection that if you knew something, it was all right to repeat it. By the time I was ten, I had wrapped up the family title of "mouth on a trolley." Father named me best in class on a trip to New York, where he was holding a sales meeting. After an all-day session, he invited one of the regional sales managers up to the suite. I loved the man's name—Ruby Katz. I had heard it often. Father made the introductions and Mr. Katz said how pleased he was to meet me because he had heard so much about me. I said I had heard a lot about him, too, and from what I'd heard, he ought to start looking for a new job. Father turned white and stammered that I had confused his name with someone else"'s and was given to making things up, anyway. When the guest had gone, Father swore for the thousandth time that he would never talk business in front of me again.

He forgot. Not long after, we were out for dinner in Eau Claire with a gang of Presto people. As usual, I was the only child present. Mel Cohen came into the restaurant carrying a suitcase. Mel Cohen, you should know, (a) worked for Presto, (b) was the son-in-law of the president of the company, "Uncle Louie," and (c) hated to travel. Shoving his suitcase in a corner, Mr. Cohen sighed that he hoped he would be in town for a good long time. "Don't unpack your bag," the little voice told him, "Father's sending you away again."

Recreation, for me, was what it had always been. Talking. It was no accident that when our class took a field trip to WEAU, the major radio station in town, I struck up a conversation with the afternoon DJ, Bob Montgomery. He invited me to drop by someday after school. When I did, we talked on the air for about half an hour between records. I was invited back yet again, and before long my on-the-air visits to *Monty's Music Shop* were a regular thing. I don't know what I thought radio was, but I often told "secrets," like how to ditch a piano lesson and go to the movies instead.

On one of these forays to be Bigmouth of the Airwaves I spotted brand-new television equipment in the next studio. They were gearing up for WEAU-TV. I wandered in to ask the station manager what shows he was going to have. He said it was a new operation and he didn't have a whole lot planned. "I'll do a show for you," I told him. I had no idea where that bit of bravado came from, but as long as I'd said it, I just kept going. "What do you do to have a show?"

"Get a sponsor."

"Will you help me?"

"No, that's not what I do."

So I went by myself to the Coca-Cola bottler, probably because he was across the street from The station. I asked if he'd like to sponsor a kid's show. Count him in for half an hour a week, he told me.

I went back to the station manager to say I'd found a sponsor. He nearly fainted. Well, what did I have in mind? he wanted to know. I said the first thing that occurred to me. I would give advice. In fact, I would ask three friends, and we would do it together.

A few weeks later, *Margo's Teenage Panel* made its debut as one of the first local shows. We very much liked the show's title because none of us was thirteen yet. the station requested letters from kids about their problems and received several. Choosing from these letters, four of us went on the air. The criteria for being a suitable panelist were that each girl speak well and be a friend of mine, not necessarily in that order.

During the show we guzzled Cokes like mad, out of gratitude, and chattered back and forth until we put together an answer to each question. I was the big cheese because I had made myself moderator, and we drew mail in sufficient quantities to make the station manager almost deferential.

If no one from *Margo's Teenage Panel* made it to the broadcasting big time, there was one WEAU-TV alumnus who did. Roger Grimsby started there as an announcer who found himself suddenly elevated to newscaster when the regular one was arrested for window-peeking.

A lot of people, mostly kids, were impressed that I had a television show. They wanted to know how I was able to solve other people's problems. "Oh, it's not hard," I always told them. "Anyone can give advice."

The real reason I felt able to give advice was that I had gotten so much. Mother had been preaching her get-your-act-together gospel from the time I was a little girl. She always knew what was right and what was not and felt an obligation to pass on this information to me. Mine was a real Hallmark mother: she had rules and opinions to fit any occasion. Following her example, consciously or un-, I was comfortable passing along my-idea/her-idea of what was correct. It never seemed hard to dope out a solution— particularly if it was for somebody else.

Mother was not only straitlaced but also liked to show off the laces. She neither drank nor smoked, and made quite a production of it. No one ever heard that she just didn't care for a drink. What they heard was that liquor was a crutch and after a few belts no one spoke a word of sense. Father called her Carrie Nation.

He, of course, drank and smoked. He wasn't smashed particularly often, he just drank a lot. No one said he was alcoholic. No one even thought it. Why would they? He was Jewish. If I were to have drawn a picture of Father when I was young, it would have been with a glass of Scotch in one hand, a Chesterfield in the other, and a telephone fastened to his ear. It is my guess that more tan one person meeting Eppie and Jules Lederer for the first time decided that, yes, opposites do attract.

They called each other "Led," for Lederer, and I was "Little Led." We must have sounded nuts in an airport. Interestingly, Mort Phillips called Mother Esther. Aside from a few older aunts, he was the only one who did. She felt there was hostility in his use of that formal name, that it was a way of distancing himself. Morton was very reserved to begin with, but his aloofness from Mother probably had to do with his closeness to Father. They worked together, traveled together, and played together. Mother and Morton felt mildly competitive, each thinking the other was lousing things up, just a little, in terms of Father's time.

Whether it was Father's absences or Mother's choice, my upbringing was almost entirely her domain. Any questions having to do with me were raised with Stolar. I therefore never thought of my parents as "the folks," but as two separate entities. She was the decision maker, disciplinarian, teacher, confidante. He was warm, loving, and Daddy. He was also Santa Claus, a great generous buyer of treats. Mother, however, did not invest his generosity with the image of Father Christmas. She thought he more closely resembled a cash register, and said so. She was sure I was living by the French proverb that says "A father is a banker provided by nature." Mother decided that the bond between Father and me was the giving and receiving of gifts. Surely, without knowing it, she was acting out her wish for perfection by subtly establishing an "us" against "them." (She and I were "us," Father was "them.") If he didn't travel so much, he could be a better father; then he wouldn't feel he had to give so many gifts. Since he wouldn't cut out the traveling, he couldn't be a perfect father.

The question of generosity—or indulgence—was, at the time, a minor problem. A major one was the twin business. After living in the same small town with Popo for seven years, Mother knew it wouldn't work. She needed a singular identity, and she couldn't have one in Eau Claire. It was simply too small a town, and she was Popo's sister.

Things were further complicated by both husbands being at Presto. Although there were some people who figured that Father was running the company, it could also be said that he worked for Morton. The connection to the Phillipses made the Lederers appear to come in second. This was not what Mother had in mind.

On another level, Popo's generosity had become oppressive. There was nothing sinister at work, it was just Popo's nature to be gifty. And perhaps she was a touch too articulate about not wanting something if Eppie couldn't have it, too. The pattern was that Popo would treat, and give, and buy with the stated purpose of wanting her twin to have whatever she had. What Mother had, after a while, was the feeling that she was the poor relative. Stolar wanted that to change.

Mother and Father toyed with leaving Eau Claire for many months. When they finally decided to move, Father had no idea what he could do next. It hardly seemed to matter. During the Presto years he had built a solid reputation, along with connections in and out of the appliance field. He understood that Mother was not just humoring him when she said he would land on his feet. If she needed to leave Eau Clare, he would do that for er.

Since Father didn't know what he would do or where he would do it, they decided to pick a city they liked and wing it. They chose Chicago. Mother and I took the Four Hundred and spent a weekend house-hunting. The house turned out to be a new high-rise at 1000 Lake Shore Drive. She signed a lease for a three-bedroom apartment. The poor relatives were moving to the big city in style. Father sold his Presto stock, which both supplied the money and completed the break. Well . . . almost. He and Morton no longer worked together, but their friendship was intact.

We moved in the summer of 1954. It was sure a different Chicago than the one we had lived in before. This time there was no Murphy bed or a secondhand Ford. Now there were doormen and taxis and traffic and elegance. I felt as though I were on another planet. Not only would I be starting a new school, but it would be high school. Will Munnecke, my old friend from the train, was drafted as educational adviser. Mother asked him to pick a school for me, and he chose Francis Parker.

I had a school before Father had a job. After weeks of sifting offers, he accepted the presidency of the Autopoint

Corporation, an advertising-specialty firm dealing mainly in ball-point pens and pencils. He turned out to be the sellingest president anybody ever saw. In fact, whenever he met someone who asked what he did, the answer was always the same: "I'm a salesman."

With Father and me squared away, Mother could now resume her hobby-career. Since she had been about to be named Democratic national committeewoman from Wisconsin, she figured she could just change her base and continue in Chicago. She figured wrong.

Going to her old friend Colonel Arvey, she asked for guidance about how to proceed. Jack Arvey was the top Democrat in Chicago politics then, even counting Mayor Daley. He didn't miss a beat in response to her question. She couldn't just pick up where she left off, he explained, because Illinois was not Wisconsin. The Chicago machine was not manned by La Follette Democrats, let alone women. "If you persist," he told her, "I will worry that you might wind up in Lake Michigan wearing a cement ankle bracelet." He was kidding. Sort of. To make sure she didn't misunderstand, Arvey gave the message to Father, as well. Mother was surprised—and a little bit stuck. She would spend months figuring out what to do with herself. But she did know one thing: she would do something.

Chapter 13

Mother knew she had a calling, she just didn't know what it was. Being shut out of politics put the kibosh on the thing she knew how to do best, but there had to be something else. The mystery occupation had no delineation in her mind, but she knew she would know it when she saw it.

She saw it one morning in August of 1955. Reading the *Sun-Times*, Will Munnecke's paper, Mother reread one of the features two or three times. It was their advice column. It said at the bottom that you could send your problem to Ann Landers and get a personal reply, even if your letter wasn't used in the paper. Mother reasoned that the woman who wrote the column must be swamped with mail and decided that here was something that would be interesting to do: helping Ann Landers answer the mail.

With half of breakfast still on the table, Mother phoned

"Uncle Will" at the office. "I've figured out what I want to do," she announced. "I'll help Ann Landers answer the mail."

There was a lengthy pause on the other end. "It is odd," Will mused, "that you are calling me now. Ruth Crowley, our Ann Landers, died suddenly last week. I'll have to call you back."

Mother's timing was startling, even to her. When Munnecke did call back, she had yet another idea. Since there was now no one to be assistant *to,* she would just take over the column. She knew it was a reach, but she had a feel for it, and so advised Munnecke. They were close enough for him to reply with candor: he laughed out loud. Sensing that there were hurt feelings on the other end, he explained that the newspaper business was not about granting wishes to ladies with sudden inspirations and nothing to do. This column, in particular, he said, called for training that Mother simply didn't have. Crowley had been both a newspaperwoman and a nurse. There was the added complication that "Ann Landers" wasn't just a local feature but was syndicated in forty papers.

Mother was not deterred. She asked how the new Ann Landers would be selected. Munnecke said they had decided to have a competition. All the contestants would be given the same letters so their answers could be compared for substance and style. A day or two later he reported that twenty-one contestants were lined up. The good news was that eighteen of them were writers and reporters, the bad news was that three of them were executives' wives. "More bad news," Mother interrupted. "Now there's another contestant. Munnecke saw no point in seeming heavy-handed and arbitrarily keeping Mother out of the contest.

It would become evident to her that she couldn't cut it, so he said, "Fine. You're in the contest." They would get rid of her, fair and square.

Mother was in swell shape to enter a competition where the prize was writing a seven-day-a-week advice column. She had never written a line for publication, and in fact had never held a paying job. She didn't know what the inside of a newspaper office looked like. Not only was she not a nurse, she was not an anything . . . .including a college graduate. Her experiences were devoid of hard knocks and she was, quite simply, a square Jewish girl from Iowa. She mentioned that I was the only thing she had going for her. "At least I can be described as a mother," she sighed.

But of course she could have been described as other things, too. She was confident—in both her judgment and her abilities. She learned quickly, had common sense and a clear idea of right and wrong. In addition to being highly motivated, she had incredible energy and amazing chutzpah. For example: one of the sample letters came from a woman inquiring about a neighbor's apples which fell into her yard. Whose were they, anyway?

Mother knew there was a legal answer to this, so she called a friend who was a lawyer. Justice William O. Douglas. She had met him in Washington with Hubert Humphrey and they had become friends. Justice Douglas was a little taken aback by the question about the apples, but he did come up with an answer. The woman could eat the apples from the neighbor's tree, or cook with them, or play with them. The only thing she couldn't do was sell them.

Moter was knocking out her sample columns in such a way that they were entertaining, authoritative, and easy to understand. There was no trick; she was just writing the way she talked. What with the breezy style, the good advice, and the heavy hitters like Justice Douglas, the judges at the *Sun-Times* were impressed . . . only, they didn't know by whom because each contestant had a code number. This bit of blind justice was necessitated by the executives' wives in the contest.

Week by week, more would-be Ann Landerses were eliminated and the survivors given new letters. The *Sun-Times* brass whittled down the group to four women. Then two. Then they made the final decision. Having made their selection, the numbers were decoded. The winner was . . . *Eppie Lederer?*

There was a small meeting with Mother and a few executives. They have her a ringing vote of confidence. "You'll never last," they told her. "This is tough stuff and nobody's going to work that hard if she doesn't need the money."

Munnecke felt she could do it, but he was the only one who knew her. The others were so skittish about their winner that they refused to give her a contract, figuring she'd fold in a matter of weeks. Mother, too, was nervous about her victory. It was like the old joke: be careful what you wish for . . . you may get it.

If I was already used to seeing Father bring home briefcases, now I could watch the two of them work. Mother set up shop in the den with a modern blond desk, an office-size IBM, and of course a telephone. Maybe it was a good omen that she had already invested countless hours in that room. What she had done was glue up her matchbook collection on two sliding doors. I remember, because I had to help, that we cut off the dark brown striking part and trimmed the sides. Mother would then glue up dozens of match covers at a time, following an angled herringbone pattern. She was working with ten years' worth of matches. To say that her collection was "colorful" was to miss the point. Looking at those doors always made me blink. Mother must have felt as I did, because she worked with her back to those doors.

The *Sun-Times* crowd was friendly and helpful and wished her well. They were also waiting for her to fall on her keester. They cheered themselves up by remembering that no one on the outside knew who Ann Landers was. It was comforting that if Mother proved unequal to the task, they could simply start to look again with the world none the wiser about their failure.

Before Mother took over the column in September 1955, it had been a dry, by-the-book, anonymously written advice column. There was certainly no personality associated with Ann Landers. There wasn't even an office. All Mother was given was a desk at the paper, toward the back of the city room. There was no secretary, no stationery, no nothing. What she did have though, was her own editor. His name was Larry Fanning. The Field brass thought if anybody could salvage the Landers column and teach this willing but inexperienced amateur to write, it was Fanning. He was then editor of the *Sun-Times* syndicate, having recently come from the San Francisco *Chronicle*, where he had become managing editor at the age of thirty-one. In a way, they were both starting together. Fanning was new to Chicago . . . Mother was new to the whole thing.

Larry Fanning was a much-loved newspaperman who was known for his integrity and class. Graduates of the Fanning blue pencil included Peter Lisagor and Mike Royko. He was serious about his business and appreciated that Mother was, too. They would spend hours a week going over copy, fighting about words, talking out concepts, articulating goals. Fanning wanted it to be a service column, not entertainment. If people got a kick out of reading it, fine, but he believed its primary function was to offer help. He did, however, nurture Mother's ability to weave in humor, but it could never be at the expense of the person with the problem. He encouraged her to rely on experts when the answer required more than common sense. He insisted she use fewer words rather than more. And he badgered her to write simply, the way people talked.

I knew what Fanning thought about Mother's work because he thought about it out loud at our apartment. His time for her at the paper was limited, and his life was such that he didn't mind spending a night or two a week working with her. She was hungry to do what she was doing better, and Fanning was so in love with newspapering that he wasn't about to close down this bright amateur with all the enthusiasm. People would wonder, later on, if he had been in love with her, but of course there was no answer.

I called him Uncle Lare, Mother called him Lare Bear, and Father called him "the Fan." He would show up for dinner and several double Scotches. He was a wonderful, slightly world-weary Irish Catholic who knew a lot of stuff and who, I think, had a sad heart. He reminded me of Gene McCarthy, the two of them wanting to be priests and baseball players. McCarthy's gift was for playing with words of his own; Fanning's was for playing with other people's.

His history was darkly romantic. He divorced his first

wife to marry a woman whose husband had worked for him at the *Chronicle*. The man was a war correspondent who was killed. In Fanning's mind it was all very clear. By assigning him to cover the Korean War, he had caused his death; he therefore would marry the widow.

Uncle Lare had two names for me: "Child" when addressing me and "the child" when referring to me. "The child" was fifteen when we met, and it was only my affection for him that allowed me to tolerate that name.

There is no way to know if Mother would have made it without Fanning. He not only taught her about newspapers and their internal politics but also defined the modern advice column. He also disabused her of any notion that she was a "journalist." She understood from the beginning that she was doing a specialized kind of writing and, to her credit, never thought of herself as Marguerite Higgins.

During those first months of writing "Ann Landers," Mother learned her way around. She dealt with choosing letters for the column, answering the ones she didn't print, putting the right letters together to make a day, and trying to organize a routine. Her days became almost indistinguishable. The better part of mornings, afternoons, and evenings was spent at the typewriter. Her uniform was a nightgown and a robe. Lunch, usually at her desk, was always the same—two soft-boiled eggs, toast, and coffee. For dessert she had several pieces of candy, preferably chocolate.

For the first six months, no one except close friends knew what she was doing. The *Sun-Times* wanted it that way. The column had always been anonymous—Mother was the third Ann Landers—and nobody saw it as the kind of column which would be enhanced by a personality.

Popo, of course, knew what Mother was doing and offered to help. Although living in the same town with her twin had proven untenable, Mother still felt close to Popo and it was natural for her to share her good news. Being determined to answer every piece of mail and having no secretarial help, Mother accepted Popo's offer of assistance. If she were willing to pitch in with the mail, Mother would teach her how.

She had Popo study the columns to get an idea of the style, approach, and even the length she used. Though Popo was lending a hand only temporarily (Mother felt sure she would eventually get a secretary), she explained the whole operation to her—how the column itself was put together, how many lines made a letter, how many letters made a day, what kinds of problems should go together, and which subjects were verboten. In 1955, VD and homosexuality were not discussed in newspapers.

After six months, *Sun-Times* officialdom realized that Mother meant business and that she could cut it, so they gave her a contract. For one year. At about the time they entered into this formal agreement, *What's My Line?* sent a query. Would Ann Landers be a television contestant? She wanted to do it. Her bosses said no.

Mother battled with them and enlisted Fanning's help. She wished to end the anonymity that surrounded Ann Landers. She believed that a faceless writer stood in the way of building an important property, that it prevented her— Eeppie Lederer—from getting the most mileage out of the column. Perhaps her connection to "the show business" and her own theatricality militated against an unacknowledged position. If she was going to do this thing, she wanted to do it center-stage.

110

Her style was so different from her predecessors' that the executives agreed it was worth a try to go the opposite way. Mother won the battle . . . .and the right to go on *What's My Line?* What happened next is enough to make a girl believe in fairy godmothers. She flew to New York Saturday morning to do the show on Sunday. Saturday night, Fred Allen died. There was a question as to whether the program would be broadcast at all. It was finally decided to go. Not only did Mother appear on television to bring Ann Landers out of the closet, but also millions of people watched who otherwise never did—just to see what would happen without Fred Allen.

The show's Hooper rating was phenomenal. If Mother was hoping that a few old friends would stumble onto her whereabouts, she was unprepared for hearing from the immediate world. I mean, she heard from people with whom she'd gone to kindergarten.

Two things were unmistakable. The identity of Ann Landers was no longer a secret, and Mother definitely had found something to do. The fact that she had taken over an "agony column" and was telling people how to straighten out their lives made perfect sense. She was opinionated, sure of herself, and not averse to minding other people's business. Luckily for this kind of work, Mother viewed the world with hardly any shades of gray. Even her liabilities turned into pluses. The square, righteous Jewish girl from a cushy Midwestern background turned out to be a better source of support and counsel than a hard-bitten reporter who might have regarded giving advice as just another assignment. For Mother, being Ann Landers was the farthest thing from a job. It was, rather,a mission . . . .a contribution to make, an identity to have. Ann Landers

111

may have been who she was all along.

Larry Fanning was to be the architect of her success as well as the maintenance man. Theirs would become a legendary newspaper association because he taught her to write and made her a star. He would edit the column and be her sounding board for twelve years, even as he changed positions within the Field organization. He went from the Syndicate to the *Sun-Times,* as executive editor, then to the Chicago *Daily News* as editor in chief. He would finally give up his involvement with the column in 1967 when he married Kay Field, the divorced wife of his boss, and moved to Alaska. He had, himself, gotten a divorce to make this new mariage.

The mainstay of the column, what Fanning called its "integrity," was service and credibility. Mother started a list of free services in the forty cities where the column appeared. When more papers were added the list was enlarged. It was amazing to her that people didn't know about Legal Aid if they had no money but needed a lawyer, or that there was free dental care available, or community mental-health counseling. In time, her list would become so comprehensive that H.E.W. was calling *her* for information.

After a while she began writing pamphlets on particular topics which readers could send for. The one I remember best was "Necking and Petting and How Far to Go." It was no small source of embarrassment for me. As a teenager I was sensitive to the gloppy aspect of her work, and that title had become something of a hilarity among my friends.

It never occurred to her, of course, that writing pamphlets, in addition to a seven-day-a-week column, was too much work. In her private life Mother was truly compulsive, so it followed that in her career she would be the same way. She could not leave a dish unwashed, a bill unpaid, or a letter unanswered. Her motivated use of time was probably the key to getting everything done. Letters to Ann Landers, for example, were read in the bathtub, under the hair dryer, on airplanes, and in automobiles. Mother was always shlepping around manila envelopes that looked as though they had been force-fed. From a sense of loyalty to "her people" she tore up letters when she was through with them. She thought it would be wrong for a stranger to accidentally discover that Annabelle H. in Peoria was having an affair with the plumber in order to get free faucet handles.

Mother's chief adviser, of course, was Stolar. If he didn't know what she needed to know, he put her in touch with someone who did. She was fond of saying that the advioce may be free to her readers but that her phone bill read like the national debt. Father and I were often drafted to give an opinion. Mother would appear with a piece of yellow copy paper marked up within an inch of its life. "Can I read to you?" she'd ask, or "Can you listen?" We sometimes made suggestions, but mostly just cheered and urged her on. Father felt Mother's new incarnation was perfect for her. He called her, with affection, "general manager of the world."

The six-month mark was a milestone in Mother's career. It was at that point she was given a contract, allowed to go public, and then faced the only competition she would ever have. Ironically, it was the only competition she had ever really had. Abigail Van Buren, "Dear Abby," made her debut. Its creator was Popo.

The Phillipses were then living in Hillsborough, outside of San Francisco. Morton hadn't stayed at Presto long after Father left.

Popo went to the *San Francisco Chronicle,* Fanning's old paper, and apparently made a pitch that if the Landers column looked like it had possibilities, there was someone who was strikingly similar in attitude, humor, and style. Her. Having, in essence, been taught by Mother how the column worked, she was well-equipped to begin one of her own. It sounded interesting to the *Chronicle* and they gave her a chance. To show that they were behind her, they dropped the advice column they already had, by Molly Mayfield.

The newspaper business was one of the few fields where such a coup was possible. Most towns in the mid-fifties had two papers. This made a competitor quite viable . . . especially one who was the twin sister of a columnist making a name for herself.

Popo became the imitator. Maybe it was their destiny to remain two. Once again the Friedman twins were a sister act, only this time the rivalry was bitter and public. The two of them were to use newspapers as a battleground. Their difficulties would become one of the all-time full-blown sister feuds.

When Popo told Mother about the *Chronicle,* the announcement was received with frosty interest. Mother voiced reservations, but sighed that things would probably be okay as long as Popo didn't become syndicated . . . which is exactly what happened three weeks later.

Mother's partisans thought the whole thing was overtly hostile and opportunistic. Father remarked that "Blood is thicker than water and it boils faster, too." The incipient war did not hurt sales, however. When a new paper signed up one of the sisters, the paper across the street usually bought the other one. A side effect of all this was that local lovelorn writers were dropping like flies. The twin advice columnists were the hot new act in the newspaper business.

Popo's approach was thought to be less serious than Mother's and more given to one-liners. For people who knew them both, this was not surprising, since Popo was acknowledged to be the funnier of the two. She, in fact, was one of the few people who could always make Mother laugh. In any case, the two of them were streamlining the advice column. Theirs was unquestionably the fresh and modernized product, said by one magazine writer to sound like "Dorothy Dix by Errol Flynn."

There were recriminations and accusations. Mother said Popo was lifting letters from her column. Popo said Mother's syndicate was selling her at greatly reduced rates. Mother said Popo's syndicate was *giving* her away. It was a mess. Mother viewed Popo's career as a competitive, me-too attack. Popo felt Mother's response was selfish and petty.

What this meant for the rest of the family was that Father and Morton had to reorganize things. They viewed the squabbling girls as . . . well, squabbling girls. Both men were sympathetic to the positions of their spouses, but protected their friendship for each other. Whereas the four of them had, in the past, met for trips and parties, now the brothers-in-law met by themselves. I, of course, seemed like a clairvoyant to Mother, since I had been fighting with Popo for years.

Chapter 14

Although Mother was hell-bent on writing what Fanning called "the best damn advice column around," she was also running a business. Within a year of her taking over as Ann Landers, the volume of mail increased dramatically—both coming in and going out—and new papers were signing up all the time. The *Sun-Times* responded in kind. They gave Mother a staff of three secretaries to handle the mail, take dictation, organize speaking engagements, book her travel, and field her phone calls. She and her "girls" organized an effective record-keeping system and ran up an annual postage bill of several thousand dollars. Mother was a corporation.

Rather than going to the paper once a week as she had in the beginning, now she showed up midafternoon every day. It was the best way she knew to instruct the girls, organize the mail, sign letters, and handle correspondence. The writing of the column was always done at home.

If Fanning taught Mother how to write, he also schooled her in newspaper politics. He felt the best way to achieve control as a syndicated property was to establish rapport with editors. To do this, Mother began attending newspaper conventions, accepting invitaions to give speeches in towns that carried the column, and generally keeping in touch. Once there was a personal relationship with an editor, it was easy to request that her column be moved, (sometimes from the funny pages), that she appear above the fold rathe than below, or that they run a new picture. Mother thought it important to be recognized, and a good way to be recognized was to run a current picture. She was therefore hard at work developing photographers.

Mother was becoming to newspaper readers what Bob Stolar was to her. She couldn't have been more serious about the responsibility of answering questions and solving dilemmas. She had read *Miss Lonelyhearts* and wept and learned from her mail that people could get themselves into unbelievable situations. She became respectful of the fact that life can deal terrible cards. She got used to readers telling her to drop dead, get lost, stop playing God, and quit making up those nutty letters. She was often asked how she had the gall to tell people what to do with their lives—in a paragraph, yet—after hearing only one side of the story. In time, Mother became comfortabe with these broadsides. The letters that passed through her hands taught her that people who wrote to a newspaper for help were those who had nowhere else to turn. Often they were people who could not afford professional help or had no friendly shoulder to cry on. Sometimes they were simply too embarrased to confide in anyone they knew or too

shy to talk to a stranger. The anonmity of an unsigned
letter was as close as they were going to get to asking for
help. Early on, Mother developed a gut-level empathy for
"her people." The temperature of a conversation could drop
precipitously if anyone opened a mouth about "the jerks
who write to a newspaper."

There were those who dismissed Mother's work as a bit
of fluff which required little effort. They were sure that
"half the work was done by the goofs who write in." This
perception was only to ignore the task of reading thousands
of letters, selecting suitable material for the column,
trimming length, fixing grammar, and laundering language. Then there was the actual process of formulating the
advice, whech often entailed conferring with an expert.

With Stolar always in the background, Mother developed a group of top people in different fields who were
happy to offer assistance. Some of the experts she knew.
The ones she didn't she called up anyway . . . and then she
got to know them. People who were accomplished seemed
happy to help, maybe because Mother communicated her
belief that what she was doing was important.

The way she worked was to do four or five drafts of a
column by herself, then work it over with Fanning. He
frequently tossed copy back at her with remarks such as
"The advice is too tough," "It's not tough enough," or
"Funny, but not helpful."

Mother was on her way to becoming famous. Public
appearances were frequent, and she packed them in at
lectures. She was also one of the few columnists who could
be read 365 days a year. She liked to quote Red Smith on
the subject. "Writing a daily column is easy. All you have
to do is sit at the typewriter untill small drops of blood

form on your forehead." It was Fanning's decision that she run seven days a week, not five. It was another way to have control. If you didn't take vacations in print, including Saturdays and Sundays, there was less chance of another columnist filling your space. The nature of the column, as well, demanded continuity. Advice and problems seemed to hook readers in a way that political commentary did not.

Mother's discipline was extraordinary and her column was turning into a newspaper phenomenon. The list of papers that carried Ann Landers just kept growing. Mother would topple the readership records of Will Rogers, O.O. McIntyre, Walter Winchell, and Dorothy Dix.

Father was exceedingly proud of her achievement, and I was . . . . unconsciously. I was too old, as a child, to be much affected, and too young, as an adult, to be impressed. I was occasionally embarrassed, perhaps, because as a teenager I thought there were more impressive things to be than an advice queen. I was also bored by the clever question "Do *you* ask your mother for advice?" But mostly it didn't matter one way or the other. The column was just something she did, and the thing I liked best about it was that it deflected her energy and intensity away from me. I thought it a fair excange that her Jewish-mother tendencies were refracted from me to the newspaper-reading public.

Because Mother started writing when I was fifteen, I was spared growing up as the little girl of a famous mother. We had talked about this and concluded we had been lucky, that we had beaten the rap of the famous-parent/over shadowed-child. There weren't even the attendant pitfalls that come with comparisons. It wasn't as though she was beautiful and I was plain or that she was brilliant and I was backward. To my knowledge, no one ever said, "Oh, too bad. The kid's a yo-yo." As for wondering if my friends liked me for reasons that had nothing to do with me, that was never a possibility because I had made friends in Chicago before Mother was a celebrity—and I kept the same friends. This is not to say that I had no problems, just that Mother's public identity wasn't one of them.

If Father was proud of her career and I was indifferent, Will Munnecke was just terribly pleased. He had become the accidental hero in her success. Mother dubbed him "the world's number-one number-two man" for his having been a vice-president of Marshall Field & Company as well as of the University of Chicago. When I found him on the train, he was already vice-president of the Field papers.

Will and Sis had a summer home in Traverse City, Michigan, which my folks found charming. They were so taken with the community and the aura of relaxation that they bought a house there for weekends. It was a contemporary A-frame set in a white-birch forest with a fast-moving little river running through the property. Of course there was an IBM electric in the spare bedroom. Mother could not be away from Chicago for even a weekend without being able to work.

Just as other women would take along a good book or a half-knit sweater on holiday, so Mother would schlepp envelopes full of other people's problems. She and Father were so busy, however, that it became an effort to take themselves away to relax. The visits to Traverse City diminished. Father figured if he amortized the price of the house, each weekend cost him $15,000.

Chapter 15

A nice idea, a weekend place, but not particularly useful. Since neither one of them liked to relax, they didn't need a special house to do it in. Chicago was where they really lived and that was what they liked. Our apartment was quite like Mother—bold and to the point. The furniture was modern and the colors were Christmas and chiaroscuro—red, green, black, and white. There was a lot of marble and velvet and patterned wallpaper featuring metallic foil backgrounds. The whole place looked as though it had been designed by Mies van der Rohe in the throes of delirium tremens.

If Mother's splurge was the apartment (which she did all by herself), Father's was a new business. In addition to running Autopoint, he opened a ball-bearing factory in Puerto Rico. When it started to cost him money and sleep, he unloaded it at a loss. Whether he was making it or losing it, money was what Father was about. He found it easily more interesting than anything else he could think of, and acknowledged that for him it was the only game in town. He was not without humor on the subject. At a Young Presidents convention in Miami (a group that is exactly what it sounds like), Father went to their "Suppressed-Desire Ball" wearing slacks and a shirt completely covered with dollar bills. His desire? To be made of money. He received honorable mention. First prize, however, went to Dumas Milner, who owned a Chevrolet agency. Milner, a funny Southerner, came in street clothes with a donkey in tow: his desire was to get his ass thrown out of the Fontainebleau.

If the Young Presidents Organization was compatible with Father's night-and-day interest in business, so was his new hobby . . . collecting money. A friend instructed him in the buying of uncirculated coins and mint proof sets. While some of this collection was stored in a bank, several closets at home held boxes of new pennies, nickels, and dimes. On occasion, if I was stuck, I would use a tiny part of the collection to get on a bus.

Mother was a complementary partner to Father when it came to money. He earned it, she invested it. He had no interest in what it could buy; she did. While she wasn't nearly as free about giving me money as he was, she talked a lot about how to use it and how to invest. She was less nouveau than he, if only by one generation.

One of Mother's interests was the stock market. If her theories were ditsy now and then, the results were spectacular. Basically she made decisions by listening to the heads of companies and evaluating them—as people.

*   *   *

If Mother was running the world, someone had to run the house. Willie Washington was hired about the time Mother started writing and she is there today. Eventually there was a chauffeur—who was hired for an interesting reason. After living in Chicago for two years, Father actually saw Mother drive her own car. He watched her pull out of the garage and said it wasn't fair to other people to have her behind the wheel. Mother rather liked this new way of getting around. It meant she could sit in the backseat and read letters. For various reasons there was a procession of chauffeurs. One of them had to be let go because he drove like Mother; another could not speak English, rendering him useless on the car phone.

Mother's last housekeeping chore was to teach Willie all her recipes. This may have been a mistake. While Mother's soups were wonderfully imaginative, she was not from the great cooks. The result was that the so-so meals we were accustomed to could now be duplicated by Willie.

I was awful about food, imagining myself a deprived gourmet. After all, I could make jelly in a pressure cooker. When Father was away, Mother always let Willie go early and made dinner for us herself. She had two "just-girls" menus: one was cornflakes, fruit, and milk . . . the other was fried eggs and toast. These dinners looked suspiciously like breakfast to me, but Mother said they were nutritious and that's what counted. With all my carrying on about food, it was inevitable that I cooked my own goose. Literally. Mother decreed that I make dinner one night a week—and so I did, and learned to cook.

The general outline of our family was that there were two workaholics and me. When Father was in town, his typewriter and Mother's would be going at night. Her background music was Errol Garner, his was the TV. They both had enormous drive and energy, loving the busyness and the chance for expression. If Mother had been nudged into a career as a way of coping with Father's immersion in work, she went at it like a born-again zealot. What all this said to me was that I was the odd one because my own energy level was nearly zip. I was happy to skate by and do the minimum, believing that life was about entertaining oneself. I understood later that everyone had a different idea of entertainment, and decided that people with a need to achieve were driven by a neurotic motor. Father's need was to get away from being the boy with no money, Mother's was to outdistance a twin sister with whom she'd always been compared.

It was one of Mother's regrets that I didn't have the discipline or the motivation she had. But why would I? Everything was so comfortable. She would speculate that I might have been a go-getter if she had been stricter, or even if she had believed in corporal punishment. If I don't count the time Father wapped me for crossing a street without him when I was three, I had been hit only once. Mother and I were havig a go-round. I was fourteen. I made a brief remark: "You are crazy." She slapped my face and told me she could never have said such a thing to her mother. Then she burst into tears and asked forgiveness for the slap.

Chapter 16

The mark of who knew Mother was what they called her. She made a decision, early on, that Ann Landers was a professional name and that she was really Eppie. This was a contrast to the way Popo had chosen to go. Se became Abby to everyone, including her husband. The irony was that although Popo's identity merged into "Abigail Van Buren," her work was, I think, just her work. Mother, on the other hand, was adamant that she not be swallowed up by "Ann Landers," and yet she became her professional self in a fundamental sense, fashioning herself into a woman who had all the answers and knew all the rules.

Public-person/private-self is a cloudy area, at best. In politics, for example, Mother maintained her friendships, but while her chums in Washington called her "Eppie," they were thinking of her as "Ann." It was impossible for someone whose career turned on implicit wisdom to block out that aura in persoal relationships.

Nobody ever said Mother was wishy-washy, so it came as no surprise that she often had splenetic opinions about those in power. Richard Nixon figured in two that I know of.

When he was running for vice-president, we were in Florida at a party where he was. Someone steered him over to Mother with an opening line that went, "This is Ann Landers. I know she'll want to say 'Good luck.'" Mother laughed and said "Oh, no, I don't want tó say 'Good luck' at all, but I will say 'How do you do?'" He gave her a funny look.

The other Nixon-related gaffe was at an ASNE dinner in Washingtoń. The American Society of Newspaper Editors had Nixon as their keynote speaker. When hewas introduced, everyone stood to applaud. Predictably, Mother remained seated. The man to her right asked, over the din, why she wasn't standing. To answer him, she raised her voice considerably to be heard over the applause. The clapping abruptly stopped, however, just as Mother was heard to holler, "I wouldn't dream of standing up for that SOB." Larry Fanning was at Mother's table, laughing. His assessment of that performance was repeated often. "Eppie," he smiled, "is a stand-up dame with balls."

A familiar refrain in Mother's column was, "Discuss this with your clergyman." She got a whole new slant on things as more and more people wrote back, "I can't discuss this with my clergyman. I *am* my clergyman." Mother knew, intellectually, that everyone had problems, but clerics were somehow exempt, in her thinking. If she looked up to

Margo at age four.

Mother and Father on vacation, Mackinac Island, Michigan.

Mother, Father and I at a street fair in Chicago.

Mother and Hubert Humphrey at my first wedding, 1962.

Mother and I at one of her lectures in Clinton, Iowa. It is unclear why a sherpa was in Clinton, Iowa.

Mother in a helicopter gunship in Vietnam.

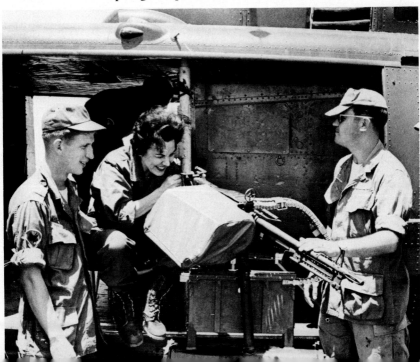

Eppie, her twin sister Popo (Abigail Van Buren), and friend.

Mother and Father (*right*) with Popo and her husband, Morton Phillips.

Mother and Father.

When my children were young.

Mother, playing up her role
as grandmother.

Father comforting Adam.

Mother and President Jimmy Carter at O'Hare.

With my husband Ken Howard in our California home.

clergymen and assigned to them other-wordly goodness, what, then, was she to make of their predicaments? This blind spot may have come from a wish to believe in perfect people—and priests were as close as she could get. They did, after all, work for God.

Father Hesburgh would become one of her closest friends. They met at a Young Presidents seminar in Pheonix; then, as now, Ted Hesburgh was president of Notre Dame. Mother came to regard him as a spiritual adviser even though his religion had nothing to do with hers—at least for the last two thousad years. Perhaps he was an ecclesiastical version of Stolar.

If Bob Stolar was not the most perfect person Mother knew, he was certainly the one with the most impact. It was he who weaned her away from being one of "the twins," strongly encouraged her to leave Eau Claire, and often restated the goal that she achieve something on her own.

Mother assigned to him almost mystical powers of understanding and figured if he had been good for her, he would be good for me. Which is why, my senior year in high school, Bob and I were talking on the phone— Chicago to Washington—two or three times a week for about an hour in the evening. Mother's idea. We were going through that sticky time of teenage girls and their mothers with the competitive feelings and the ill will. I complained that she was busy being girlish with my friends, she thought I was self-centered and unmotivated. The usual. I wanted to see a "real" doctor, but Mother said no, Bob would be fine. Her position was that I didn't need psychiatric help just a little "support." If this posture seemed to fly in the face of her oft-stated advice to "get professional help," it was probably because I was a blind spot for her as well as an iffy candidate for therapy. If I had been writing on the walls with crayons, I doubtless would have been put with a "real" doctor promptly.

One of my difficulties with Mother was my reaction to how she sometimes functioned—or didn't. I felt she wasn't wrapped real tight about things I considered elemental. How, for example, could she foul up written instructions? For reasons known only to Freud, her impairment usually surfaced when it came to going somewhere. She would read Tuesday for Wednesday, transpose a departure time into a flight number, or have herself met at the wrong airline. I remember one incident, in particular, because I was with her and the mistake took up two days. We went to the DiSalle wedding in Columbus. Mother, Mike, and Myrtle DiSalle were friends from political days and Mike DiSalle was then governor of Ohio. One of the DiSalle daughters was being married, so we went to Columbus for the wedding. Father had the good fortune to be elsewhere.

When we landed, Mother called their house. "We're here," she chirped. "You're where?" Myrtle inquired tentatively.

"At the Columbus airport," Mother replied.

"Well, come on over," Myrtle instructed.

We got tothe governor's residence, where I was a nervous wreck to find that two lifers from the state penitentiary were serving as household help. It was a special interest of Governor DiSalle's to rehabilitate those in the slammer. Well, it turned out that the wedding was actualy the following Saturday, so we all had dinner, stayed the night, and the loonies flew back to Chicago the next day. Gracious about the error I was not. There is no one so unforgiving about missteps as a teenager who fancies herself perfect.

Mother, alas, was not able to overcome this short circuit in her thinking. She once had Phil Donahue—live—talking aobut his laundry while he waited for her to be driven to his studio at WGN after first showing up at ABC. The polarity was that she was going there to be the practical, organized Ann Landers, but the person instructing the driver was a slightly confused Eppie.

Chapter 17

Television served Mother well. She related to live audiences easily — they were, after all, "her people." Ann Landers and her Iowa twang were much in demand. She was an original without the polished suavity of a performer. In those early years she hardly ever said no to a television show. The old song was right: How ya gonna keep 'em down on the farm, once they've done *What's My Line?* Popo, of course, was on the same circuit, a touch more theatrical, with an instinct for the double entendre. Some people confused them . . . just like old times.

Toward the end of 1957, the feud between the twins was at its most feverish. Mother felt Popo was playing so fast and loose with the facts—and the numbers—that something needed to be done. If Mother said in interviews that she got two thousand letters a week, Popo said she was receiving seven thousand. If Mother stated she had 150 client papers, Popo said the Abby clients numbered 300. Because it wasn't all that difficult to determine whose column was carried where, Mother and her syndicate knew they were being hyped.

In the syndicate business everybody famously inflates his numbers. It is the newspaper version of virility. Mother maneuvered her syndicate into doing the unheard-of: running an ad in *Editor & Publisher,* the newspaper trade magazine, naming Ann Landers' clients. There were 180 of them at the time.

The unpleasantness between the twins was resolved shortly thereafter. The resolution did not end the war, merely the communication. Mother advised Popo that she wished to stop all phone calls, letters, and visits. Their older sisters, of course, were horrified. It was unheard-of — twin sisters not speaking. Father and Morton hunkered down and waited for the dust to settle. I, a senior in high school, didn't care much one way or the other.

Then I cared. In April 1958 *Life* magazine did a story about the feud. It read like an updated version of the Hatfields and the McCoys if they had been rich and famous. What had previously been family business was now being discussed wherever people liked good gossip. The cover of that *Life* magazine was ironic. It featured Carmen Basilio and Sugar Ray Robinson. Maybe it was their fight issue.

Paul O'Neil, a senior writer for *Life,* did the story. He all but moved in with us for four days and brought a photographer with him. They would arrive before breakfast and leave when it was time for bed. I felt quite comfortable with O'Neil, my only adjustment to his presence being that I didn't smoke in front of him. This was no great hardship because I didn't smoke in front of Mother, either.

There were no good-news/bad-news jokes in those days, but if there had been, the *Life* piece would have been one. The good news was that they devoted eight pages, with pictures, to Mother, Popo, and their families. The bad news was what was written in those eight pages. O'Neil had simply let the twins snipe at each other and, in so doing, produced one of the more horrendous pieces about sibling rivalry since Jacob and Esau, which had been written about elsewhere. It seemed that every terrible thing Mother and Popo thought about each other found its way into print.

The title of the piece was "Twin Lovelorn Advisers Torn Asunder by Success." O'Neil spoke of "the wildly competitive female twins" who were "terse and entertaining." To entertain his own readers, he chose a selection of "snappy samples" from each:

Abby: "What is the cure for a man who has been married for 33 years and still can't stay away from other women?" Answer: "Rigor mortis."

Ann: "I'm a mail carrier and my job starts at 8 A.M. This is time enough for women to get a dress on and run a comb through their hair. Most housewives look so terrible it's enough to spoil a man's day." Answer: "You ain't never been a woman at eight o'clock in the morning."

After O'Neil gave his opinion that "each has the sort of lush figure which seems designed primarily for slithering through beaded curtains," he talked about the dual domestic scene, as he perceived it. "Despite their aggressiveness and their frank need for personal success, they talk tirelessly and glowingly about their husbands. Abby calls her husband 'loveboat' in public and smooches him in restaurants. Ann carries marital self-abnegation so far that

135

she has had the legend 'Jules' wife' rather than her own initials sewn inside her dark mink coat and blue mink stole."

He remarked on the twins' similar work habits—how they both worked long hours and lugged handbags full of letters with them, and that although

Neither finds time to read much of anything else, Abby does keep a tome entitled *The Hostile Mind* on her bedside table and occasionally consults it for clues to what she considers Ann's inexplicable behavior. Both find it hard to stay away from their typewriters. "If I had to leave the column for even a day or two," says Ann, "I know I'd feel anxious about it." For all the light tone they achieve, each feels that she is fulfilling an important mission in life. But the evidence indicates that it is their subtly ferocious personal struggle which lends their work its real fascination, and that without this goad neither of them would ever have begun it in the first place. For years, Ann says, she has been trying to get her twin back. "I understand why she's disturbed," Abby says. "She wanted to be the first violin in the school orchestra, but I was. She swore she'd marry a millionaire, but I did." She adds innocently, "I'm not trying to be the champion. It's just like playing poker. If you don't *have* to win, you get the cards, and she's always just had to win. But I love her." Ann replies: "That's her fantasy. She's just like a kid who beats a dog until somebody looks, and then starts petting it."

*   *   *

There were a few side effects from that article which had little to do with the battle of the twin sisters. (1) We learned that a lot of people have no idea what they are reading. A startling number of friends checked in with, "Gosh, that was a great story in *Life*." That response was a little like witnessing a hair-pulling contest, then complimenting one of the combatants on her lovely sweater. (2) Someone incidental to the story came away with a nice compliment. O'Neil wrote that Mother had "a precociously bright 18-year-old daughter," and Popo had two children —16 and 13. (3) The article finished Mother's relationship with Fulton Sheen. She experienced a small lapse of judgment when discussing their friendship. She told O'Neil: "Bishop Sheen is one of the greatest men I've ever met, but he'll be a Jew before I'm a Catholic." The relationship was never to be repaired.

While the *Life* piece did not cause the trouble between Mother and Popo, it certainly gave an up-to-the-minute account of it to millions of people. The twins literally did not speak for years. Mother remembers it as five; I think it was ten. I was fascinated that five years, to her, seemed somehow less radical. My dear, that's all the time it took for World War II.

Chapter 18

Mother had a great deal to do with my choice of a college—and she probably got me in. Although I wasn't hopelessly backward, neither did my name come up as a National Merit Scholar. Mother decided to subtly lend a hand by asking two chums to be my references. Never did a B student get such a swell sendoff. Testimonials to my keen mind and good character came from Justice William O. Douglas and Senator Hubert Horatio Humphrey. I regarded all this as only fifty percent fraudulent because Hubert could honestly say he knew me.

The magic did not work everywhere, however. My fallback school, the University of Pennsylvania, turned me down flat and Vassar put me on the waiting list. Only Brabdeis and Sarah Lawrence took me on the straightaway.

Mother was lobbying for Brandeis. She worried that Sarah Lawrence was too close to New York and that I would major in Bergdorf Goodman. She also felt it was crucial that I be at a school that had grades and exams, which Sarah Lawrence did not. What she left unsaid was that Brandeis seemed to her like another shot at Sunday school. Maybe with a student body which was more than ninety percent Jewish I would finally learn something about my religion.

With wistful regret at giving up the chance to go to a school that had neither grades nor exams, I accepted Brandeis' kind offer and prepared as any conscientious student would. I shopped for cashmere sweaters.

When I got there I found a ten-year-old university without a whole lot of rules. You could pretty much do what you wanted. The emphasis was on smart, and there were few restrictions; all they asked was that there be no cohabiting in the student union and that undergraduates bury their own dead. I lived in Shapiro Hall at a university some of us defensively called Brand X. It was Grossinger's with textbooks, and I loved it.

My first friend was Marty Peretz, a senior who was head of orientation week, editor of *The Justice,* and student-government president. He was certainly nothing to look at, but, boy, was he smart. He took me under his wing and taught me about books. I told him as a favor I'd keep it quiet, but it was he who educated me. He also chose my major, American civilization, with Max Lerner. Marty was Max's protégé, and the three of us spent a lot of time together. . . enough so that people thought *I* was the protégée. This was not correct in any academic sense. Max kept the two of us around for entirely different reasons. Marty was brilliant; I was blond.

It was well-known at school whose daughter I was. I dealt with Mother's column the only way that seemed sensible. I denied ever reading it. "That stuff," I told people, was intellectually beneath me. I was becoming rather pretentious and liked to casually mention that I was reading James Joyce's *Useless*.

If I was mishearing the names of literary classics, I was not hearing anything at all about more technical subjects. I failed physical science, a freshman requirement, three years in a row. It made no sense to me, so I didn't go to the class. Mother was very good about this, probably because it made no sense to her, either. She was not in a good position to carp, actually, because she had told me about her song: Don't blame me for flunking geometry. . .

The first time she came to school was when she gave a speech in Boston. She seemed quite like a visiting movie star—with dark glasses and a mink coat, greeting every-one—until we got to my room. Talking with my roommate and me she spied my laundry baghanging on the back of the door. She walked over, got it down, and sorted out what could be washed by hand. Then she went to our little sink and did laundry. My roommate was spellbound, but it was old-hat to me. This was entirely in keeping for Mother, who had always been compulsive about getting things done. When I was younger and didn't get to a task quickly enough, she would just do it herself. If she was in someone's kitchen, having coffee with a friend, she'd begin washing the coffee-pot, her cup and saucer, whatever was around, the minute she was through. Whoever else was still sipping coffee got the idea that maybe time was up.

Father came to visit, too, whenever business took him to Boston. The two of them were traveling so much in those years that it became a neurotic habit for me to check who was where whenever there was a plane crash. Although they were fatalistic about planes (Father said if the pilot would go, he would), all their moving around was a source of anxiety for me. . . . probably because, when I was young, Mother repeatedly told me what was in her will, should anything happen to her and Father at the same time. I was not to go to any of Father's or her sisters, but to Bob and Frances Stolar. At the age of eighteen, of course, custody hardly mattered, but my thought pattern was set, the fear was ingrained.

When I went away to school, Mother informed me of another portion of her will. Probably because I was reaching an age when it was possible I might marry, she stated the she and Father had no wish to subsidize a son-in-law; therefore they were leaving all their money to charity. The point of this bogus announcement, she told me years later, was she didn't want someone to marry me for my money, and if I thought I didn't have any then such a thing couldn't happen. I therefore assumed that everything they had was going to Radio Free Europe and that I was on my own. The only exception, however, to no finanial assistance from home was if I married a young man in medical school: then she would help. This was truly a Jewish mother, but one with a twist. Her message was not "Marry a doctor so he can take care of you," but "Marry a doctor and *I* will take care of you."

Mother may have been thinking about my getting married more than I was, because she made the rule when I went to college that I could date only Jewish boys. Her explanation was that marriage was tough enough without

142

introducing religious differences. The only thing stranger than her rule was that I was following it. This put me in the odd position of basically being on my own, living away from home, but phoning up every now and then for dispensation. It never occurred to me I could do what I wanted, because my training had been to do what she wanted. I was not always scrupulous, however, about getting the dispensations. There was the time I was fixed up with the Aga Khan. I wasn't about to pass that us, but neither did I want to disobey Mother. What I did was call and explain that there was an exchange student at Harvard, his name was Khan, and what did she think? "Sounds okay to me," she said, and that was that.

Mother was simple ethnocentric. She made it a point to tell everyone she was Jewish and often mentioned it in the column. She taught Yiddish expressions to all her Gentile friends. Larry Fanning, a real Mick, was an apt pupil. So was her editor after him, A WASP named Dick Trezevant, whom she called Trezl. It occurred to me that because she was so busy being Jewish, perhaps she was ambivalent about it. I thought of her closest friends, and except for Bob Stolar, there wasn't a Jew in the bunch. Her dearest girlfriend was Blondie Brigham, the ultimate *shiksa;* then there were Will Munnecke, Hubert Humphrey, Larry Fanning, Dick Trezevant, and Ted Hesburgh. . . . and it was often remarked that Father didn't look Jewish.

Of course all this attention to Jewish made for some missteps. Mother decided, for example, that Herblock the gifted political cartoonist, should have a nice Jewish wife— and for years she told him she would find him one. She was floored when his brother died in Chicago and was told the wake would be at St. Somebody's. Why, she asked Herb, would his brother have a wake? "Because we're Catholic," he told her. Not one to take no for an answer, Mother told him she was still going to find him a nice Jewish girl because they made wonderful wives.

Chapter 19

After a year at Brandeis, Harvard summer school seemed like the place to be. I was redoing myself in the image of an intellectual, and Cambridge was the perfect setting. Mother and Father were elated, imagining that my interest was shifting from Bonwit-Teller to Hegelian theory. I signed up for a full program and would have proceeded to a studious summer had it not been for an invitation I received to Hyannis. It was a tough call—the Cape versus erudition—but I made the choice. I unregistered at Harvard, got back a sizable refund, and refinanced my summer. I neglected to tell Father that I had changed my plans, and I couldn't tell Mother because she had gone to Russia.

She decided to go there to write her first straight newspaper piece. It would be a series about the people and the country, from a human-relations point of view. In 1959 Russia was not a popular tourist spot, and Mother thought whatever she could learn would be fresh enough to be worthwhile.

She took a crash course at Berlitz to get ready. She made rapid progress in conversational Russian, having heard it spoken as a child. Mother thought it was important to have some knowledge of the language because the Soviet government was totally in charge when it came to tourists. She felt she could get better information if she were not entirely dependent on what an interpreter chose to pass on to her.

During that period, and even into the 1960's, Russian policy permitted Americans to visit only those institutions which had to do with their own work. Mother, therefore, was officially limited to visiting a newspaper. She did not go to Russia, however, to visit a newspaper, so she looked for ways to circumvent the rules. She found them.

Introduced to Harold Berman, a Harvard Law School professor, Mother asked why he was there. He told her he was arguing the Conan Doyle estate. The Russians never paid royalties, and he had won permission to bring suit. Mother finagled it so she could accompany him to court, posing as his wife. He lost, of course, but Mother got to attend a trial. She also "married" a German psychiatrist whose wife complained one night at dinner of having to visit one mental institution after another. Mother said she would love to go, and she did. The hospital was run by Dr. Leon Gendelvitch, who announcd to his foreign visitors that there was less mental illness, on a percentage basis, in Russia than in any other country in the world, simply because the government solves all the problems and provides for all the needs. Mother promptly set him straight, informing him that mental-health specialists had known for a long time that most emotional problems were in no way related to economic pressures. And as she reported to her readers, the German psychiatrist whispered to a colleague, "Does this man think we are plumbers?"

As befitted an Ann Landers account of the Crimea, mother found a way to humanize the threatening foreign country to her readers back home.

What are the Russian people troubled about? As I suspected: Ivan is worried about Irena's supervisor at the furniture factory. He has heard rumors—and she has been coming home quite late. Trina in concerned about Alexander's excessive drinking. He missed two days' work last week. The Doctorovitches are worried about their son Thomas. He is depressed about failing his exams and has lost fifteen pounds in two months.

Ludmilla and Serge are in love and want to marry but they must wait at least two years for an apartment. Elina has a lecherous boss. Igor hates his mother-in-law. The problems of people are the same the world over. In Moscow they have Russian dressing.

Not many people would go knocking on doors in Russia to see how people lived, but Mother did, and she took with her a physician from Buffalo, Wyoming. They picked an apartment building within walking distance of the hotel. Choosing a door at random, the doctor knocked, a woman opened it, and Mother made the introductions. *"Z-dros-voy-*

tyeh-Americansky nyet poney-myeh-horrashaw Paroosky." She knew this was risky business, imagining herself opening her door to two Russians who announced, "Good evening. We are Russians and we don't speak good English." The family, by now all at the door, were thrilled to see *Americansky* and invited the visitors in. To celebrate friendship, the host got out a bottle of vodka. Fearing that refusal of the drink would be misunderstood, Mother made a fast decision to accept it and drink it. Eighty-proof vodka was no joke for a woman who didn't drink, but she tried mightily to concentrate on the conversation, although she was seeing four of everybody. Once back at the hotel, she slept for thirteen hours.

Mother wrote of that hotel in her articles:

> It was a shock for which I was unprepared. It is the newest and the swankest hotel in the Soviet Union. The Ukraine Hotel took four years to build, opened in 1957, and I wouldn't be surprised if it collapsed next week. A Danish contractor put it this way: "Russians are graph-happy. Everything must go *up*. Khrushchev has ordered a crash building program. They don't care how they slap things together, so long as the bricks are on top of each other and it looks big.

Mother noted that there were one hundred grand pianos in that hotel but not a single wastebasket or a piece of writing paper. Also, that her accommodations—at $35 a day—included room, bath, three meals, car, chauffeur, and interpreter, and that "The twin beds were covered with bilious rayon spreads—the kind my mother used to throw over the porch furniture when she stored it in the attic."

From a personal bias, no doubt, the phone system interested her.

> The phone on my night table is purely
> ornamental. There is no hotel switchboard and the
> dial looks like this: A,B, an upside-down L, a Mah-
> Jongg tile, E, two K's back to back, an N
> backwards, K, and a Hebrew gimmel. Russian hotel
> rooms do not have phone books. However, this is no
> great deprivation, since the last Moscow phone book
> was published in 1951, and all numbers were
> changed in 1957. So who needs a switchboard?

In her second dispatch she was ostensibly writing about the hotel. Having been given three hangers in her closet, Mother went into the corridor looking for a maid.

> In my very best Berlitz Russian I asked, "May I
> have some hangers, please?"
> "You have hangers," was the reply.
> "Only three . . ."
> "How many does one person need?" she snapped.
> "I would like ten."
> "Money spoils people," she replied authoritatively.
> I decided things had gone far enough. "Never
> mind the political lecture, just get the hangers." In
> three minutes I had ten hangers.

Mother's advice to me if I ever went to the Soviet Union was to skip Berlitz because I could make do with one phrase: *nyet raboteh.* "It doesn't work." Except for the hidden microphones, Mother said nothing did.

From that trip she wrote a series of twelve articles, which

was distributed by her syndicate. It was a respectable piece of work for someone used to writing 600 words a day. Her observations, of course, had the same texture that her column did; the outlook, the humor, the language, were unmistakably hers.

For example, this excerpt about a Russian restaurant:

> I ordered a bowl of borscht and got one of the
> major shocks of the trip. No beets. I thought
> perhaps the waiter had misunderstood the order.
> "You wanted borscht," he said, "This is borscht."
> "Where are the beets?" I asked.
> "You want beets in your borscht, go to Poland.
> Here we use cabbage."

She reported that "Russian pastry made me suspect a conspiracy between the pastry chefs and the dentists. It's hard as granite and a threat to bridgework."

> The most fascinating aspect of a Russian
> restaurant meal is the atmosphere. There is always a
> fight in the kitchen. Loud, unrestrained arguing
> among the employees is a familiar part of the scene.
> I noticed this not only among waiters, but elevator
> girls, hotel maids, luggage porters, and salespeople.
> There seems always to be an intramural rhubarb, and
> no one is embarrassed about it.

When Mother returned from Russia, and I from "Harvard," I didn't have the heart to tell her that I hadn't actually gone to summer school, so I said nothing . . . except how much fun it was. A friend from Brandeis threw

Request permission to use in forthcoming book. Stop. Signed, Crane Brinton and Stuart Hughes."

Mother was very pleased. "Oh, give them permission," she said. "It's such a lovely compliment."

Chapter 20

In 1960 I was twenty, Mother had been Ann Landers for five years, and Father implemented an idea that would make him a mogul.

It is said that necessity is the mother of invention, but in Father's case Mother was the necessity. When she started writing, neither of them imagined that a newspaper column was a moneymaking proposition. They were wrong. As Mother's syndication grew, so did her income. In order not to get killed by taxes, Father knew he had to get into a business involving depreciation. He spent months asking friends what they thought of investing in cattle, real estate, heavy equipment, and leasebacks. The answer came from Morrie Mirkin, Mother's cousin, the one who had lived with the Friedmans his senior year in high school and who was like a brother to the twins. Mirkin lived in Los Angeles and was running a small operation renting secondhand cars. His target market was people on a budget. Mirkin did not, however, have the capital or the bankability to turn his little business into a big one. Father had both—along with the intuition that discounting and franchising were the new wave in business. He struck a deal with Mirkin, resigned as president of the Autopoint Company, and opened an office in Chicago. His plans were stenciled on the door: "Budget Rent-a-Car Corporation of America, Jules W. Lederer, President." The concept of the fledgling car-rental company became the logo: $5 a day, 5¢ a mile.

Father sold all the franchises personally, ditched the secondhand cars, and chummed up to the fleet manager of General Motors. He proceeded to set up the system, arrange a reservations network and sink a ton of money into advertising, which he believed to be the key. With an overheated air-travel card and a newly assembled group of employees, Father was in the rent-a-car business.

He operated like a movie tough guy. He swore at long-distance operators, chewed out subordinates, and burst into flash fires of temperament. Nevertheless, the people who worked for him were devoted, probably because he was devoted to the business. Though he was famously brusque in the office, his approach to Mother and me came from some other place in his personality. It was often remarked how soft he was when dealing with or talking about "his girls." It was also remarked that he was a bastard, a tyrant, and a genius of an idea man.

As always, his metaphor for life was business. When I would repeat myself one too many times asking for some indulgence or other, his response would be "Enough, kid. Don't you know when you've made the sale?" He often spoke of money and life. He told me nobody who lived as he did was in it for the dough . . . that money was just the way you kept score. I don't think he ever felt rich. He certainly didn't feel immortal. He often prophesied that he wouldn't live out his forties. When he'd have a few too many, he became melancholy and predicted he would die young, as his father had. He therefore put what he believed to be his last years into building Budget. The business he dreamed up with "Mirk" became his emotional center. Everything that crossed his radar bounced off that part of his brain labeled "Budget." Everything — including a visit to the Guggenheim Museum in New York. I had suggested we three go there on a break from school so I could put on the aesthetic dog.

It was a surprise when Father lingered by a Jasper Johns, since he was ignorant of and uninterested in art. It was a shock when he announced he wanted to buy it. Could this forty two-year-old man be newly bitten by the culture bug? Not exactly. He wanted the enormous painting for the outer office at Budget because the number five was repeated throughout the painting — as in $5 a day and 5¢ a mile.

He made an inquiry and established that the picture was not for sale. Well, would Mr. Johns care to paint another one using the number five? He would not.

Even without modern art in the office foyer, Budget Rent-a-Car would become a major international company. Father would make himself, Mirkin, and dozens of franchisees rich. He would also have more fun working sixteen-hour days than anyone thought possible.

When Budget hit its stride, there were two bemused observers, both friends of Father's from Young Presidents meetings. One was Earl Smalley, head of National Car

Rental, the other was Warren Avis. They both had casually discussed the car-rental business with Father around the pool at a YPO convention. They were amazed not only that "Julie" went ahead and started a rent-a-car business but also that it got so big so fast. In time, Budget would overtake National as the third-largest car renter in the world.

Chapter 21

My junior and senior years at Brandeis were unusual, by anyone's standards. I was hanging out with Max Lerner, auditing Scott's class on Trusts at Harvard Law School, going to the beauty shop twice a week, and serving as Marty Peretz' assistant for Good Works. He led me into the early civil-rights movement and signed me up as a worker for Sane Nuclear Policy which, I admit, I first thought was Saint Nuclear. The reason I had all this spare time was that a kindy doctor pronounced me frail and run-down and requested that Brandeis make me a special student carrying three courses instead of five. If graduating had never seemed important before, now it was an impossibility. I became irretrievably deficient in the credits department and happily engaged in the intellectual version of impulse buying. I just took whatever looked good.

There was no pressure from home to become Phi Beta

Kappa, although there were hints that they would have been terribly pleased to see my name on the dean's list. I wasn't aware of it then, but my resistance to putting my brain in gear and being a conventional student was my own muted version of a rebellion.

As rebellions go, mine was remarkably quiet and well-behaved. Mother and I actually got along very well. The only difference I remember having with her during my college years was when I voiced displeasure about the lack of effort put into my homecomings. I would fly to Chicago at the start of a vacation and there would be no particular acknowledgment that the student princess had returned. Mother would answer the door wearing a nightgown, robe, and slippers. I thought this getup bespoke indifference to my arrival and said so. I must have been adorable. When I aired my grievance, Mother said nothing.

The next time I returned to Chicago, arriving at about eleven in the morning, Mother greeted me at the door wearing a floor-length black lace gown, pearls, diamonds, and a chinchilla wrap casually draped over one shoulder. Oh, yes, and a rhinestone tiara of major proportions. Her makeup was flawless and her hair freshly done. It is hard to remember who had the last laugh. We sat down together to a bowl of cornflakes to celebrate the festive lunch-hour homecoming.

I left Brandeis in the middle of my senior year. I did not have a degree, I had a receipt. The schools's president, Abram Sachar, sent my parents a dropout's condolence note: do not feel unhappy, he wrote, that Margo won't graduate, because she has been "a real addition to the school, and the loveliest ornament we've ever had."

Ornament. I was livid. For three and a half years I had been parading around as an intellectual and he comes up with the ornament line.

My exodus from academia in December was necessitated by the need to plan a May wedding. Everything seemed to point to leaving school early and getting married: immaturity, impatience, and not enough credits to graduate. I decided then that marriage was the next logical step, probably because my parents provided a good model. My image of their marriage had been formed by little things— mostly romantic—things like watching them dance together in the living room to a phonograph record, hearing Father refer to Mother as "heaven eyes," and knowing that when he was traveling he would call her every night from wherever he was in the world.

My only miscalculation, alas, was my choice of a groom. Mother and Father pleaded, begged, and threatened that I not do this thing. He was the wrong one, they said, and would bring unhappiness such as I had never known. We could agree on nothing. My ability to withstand the pressure convinced me that I was doing the right thing. I was determined that I would marry John B. Coleman from Boston. If Mother felt my choice was deranged, at least I had obeyed her cardinal rule: although Coleman was adopted, his family was Jewish . . . and rather kosher, at that.

When it was clear that I could not be dissuaded, Mother and Father accepted my decision and pretended everything was fine. Coleman and I were married on Mother's Day, 1962. There were two rabbis, sixteen hundred azalea plants, doves in cages, rose petals in baskets, seven violinists in addition to a full orchestra, wire-service coverage, and 350 best friends. There could have been an editors' and publishers' meeting for all of them that were present, as well as a Democratic caucus led by Hubert and Muriel Humphrey.

The festivities were held in the Guildhall of the Ambassador. Mother and Father were wonderful hosts, forgetting for the moment that they didn't care for the groom. I noticed that Popo wore white—a competitive color choice, I thought. I must not have had a whole lot to think about in those days.

Mother felt the wedding was a tough ticket and therefore evaluated regrets carefully. No-shows were unthinkable. One invitee, a prominent businessman, found something better to do on the day of the wedding and canceled that morning. Mother wrote him the following note.

> Jules and I were very disappointed when you, at the last moment, were unable to be with us on our great day.
>
> It was with a heavy heart that I removed your place card from the table. I had you seated between Father Theodore Hesburgh, president of Notre Dame University, and Senator Hubert Humphrey. I had told them both so much about you that they were eager to see this fabulous guy.
>
> We do understand that at the last minute things happen, and we wanted you to know that even though there were 350 lovely people at the wedding, we missed you.
>
> Warm regards,
>
> Eppie

Mother sent me a carbon of that letter, with a handwritten note at the bottom: "This should settle his hash. The idea of having his secretary phone Sunday at noon!"

The groom and I went on a honeymoon trip to Spain and Portugal, a gift from my folks. For two weeks in Majorca I ate only gazpacho, sardines, and toast. My selections had nothing to do with any craving, they were simply due to the fact that the kitchen had an uncontrollable urge to fry everything—even the lettuce. I was getting the uncomfortable feeling that everything was fried on that trip. Everything and everybody. This was when I began to realize that I might have made a mistake.

I was, however, married, and trying to make the best of it. With hindsight it seems clear that my rebellion went beyond a cavalier approach to my studies.

Chapter 22

I had three children in five years. They were, of course, "the grandchildren." Abra, the first, was an only child for three years. Then came Adam, followed seventeen months later by Andrea, known from the age of six days as Cricket.

Each of their names bore the unmistakable fingerprints of my mother. Abra was named for Abe Friedman; Adam's middle name was Stolar; Cricket's formal handle was Andrea Ted — in honor of Ted Hesburgh. Mother's success in getting me to name three children after her father and two close friends can be attributed to a combination of her persuasiveness, my malleability, and the afteraffects of anesthesia.

Perhaps there was a clue as to the kind of grandparents my parents would be in their different approaches to the first birth. Mother gave instructions she was not to be notified when I went into labor, fearing that she, too, would experience the discomfort. She wished only to hear that there was a baby. When she did hear she came to the hospital to see me, tearily looked at little Abra through the nursery window, then went home and rested for two days. Father, on the other hand, got the news in Las Vegas while having breakfast, whereupon he announced the glad tidings to the entire coffee shop and dropped a silver dollar in a nearby slot, getting back twelve. He told me the kid was lucky.

Mother was not a chicken-soup grandma. She related to the children as a teacher of lessons and instiller of values. If the kids had a classic doting grandmother, it was Father. He was so crackers about being a grandparent that he sent Abra roses every month after her birthdate for a year and a half. He would call her long distance before she could talk. He never seemed happier than when he was on the floor amusing a small child. The picture I have of him in those years is of walking around with a baby who was drooling on his silk suit.

Once they were past the infant stage, Mother entertained the children at rather formal dinners. Even the younger ones were expected to contribute information, dinner-party-style, and then appear to be interested when someone else spoke. This can present problems if you're in kindergarten.

Mother's after-dinner ritual for the children was always a coloring contest, with a prize for best creation. She had a spare closet with a seemingly endless stock of art supplies, games, and toys. It was a remark on Mother's sense of therapeutic empathy that often the winner was not the kid who had done the most appealing drawing but the one most in need of a lift. If Adam was badgering Cricket, it was she who won the prize. If Abra was sulking, her blue train in the purple sunshine captured the honors. The kids had a hunch that the coloring contests at Grandma's were fixed, but they didn't mind because the prizes seemed to rotate on a more or less equitable basis.

My mother thought I was doing a wonderful job with the children, if you didn't count the areas of discipline, manners, and cultural enrichment. She found me woefully lax and permissive. Father, on the other hand, thought they were the best little people in the world and therefore gave me a perfect score.

On the few occasions when I was stuck for a sitter, it was not Mother who bailed me out, but Father. He would arrive with a briefcase and a toy or two. It wasn't only Mother's career that militated against her baby-sitting, she believed that "children are for young people" and didn't want me to count on her for tasks which were my responsibility. Mother contented herself with trying to get the children to shake hands when they met someone and developing in them some grasp of world affairs.

Washington was still Mother's favorite place to visit. Her commitment to political issues was as strong as when she was Democratic county chairman. That she was now Ann Landers simply added cachet to her opinions, and it was her pleasure to offer advice to her friends who were elected officials. She counseled them about their children, their wives, their health . . . and their roll-call votes.

Although she kept partisan politics out of the column, the connection between her work and her Washington friends was not unimportant. Her clout grew along with the number of papers that carried her column. As the most

widely syndicated columnist in the world, which her
syndicate believed her to be, she was repeatedly on the
Gallup Poll's list of "most admired women in the world"
and UPI's "ten most influential women in the United
States." Whenever she asked her readers to do something,
they did it. One such request was to let both houses in
Washington know that the folks back home wanted cancer-
research legislation. Millions of pieces of mail flooded the
Hill. More than one congressional friend called or wrote to
say a snide " thanks a lot." Chuck Percy had to hire
someone just to handle the mail.

Privately, Mother wrote letters of her own to legislators.
They were often in the spirit of this one, in 1965, to
Mississippi's governor, Paul Johnson.

Dear Governor Johnson:
    I've been reading in the newspapers that the voter-
registration tests in Mississippi are quite difficult. In
fact, when I read that my friend the Rev. Theodore
Hesburgh, president of the University of Notre
Dame, said that he didn't think the dean of the Law
School could pass the test — I got the distinct
impression that it must be rather stiff. Sooner or
later you are going to have to change those tests. I
hope it's sooner rather than later.

There was always moral muscle behind the things Mother
asked for. She needed her position to be correct because she
wanted to be able to ask again. There was some understanding of her own power which kept her from embracing
marginally interesting causes.

If she went to Washington to lobby around and keep her

hand in, she also went for the most interesting social life available. Mother would book herself in all over town so she could see as many people as possible. There would be dates for breakfast, lunch, tea, cocktails, and dinner. For good measure she used her "spare" time to march into various Senate offices for a fast chat.

These trips to Washington always yielded some wonderful bit of news or gossip . . . like the evening Max and Joanne Friedman had a party for her. Max Friedman was the Washington correspondent for the Manchester *Guardian*. Just before dessert the White House called to say that the president would like to come over. A Washington hostess could ask for no more. The gathering, mostly newspeople, along with Hubert Humphrey, held off dessert until LBJ arrived.

The memorable part of the evening came later on when the Friedmans' dog, apparently a Republican, sidled up to the president and peed on his leg. Mother said he nnever acknowledged that it happened and just kept on talking. She and Mrs. Friedman, both having witnessed the unfortunate event, quickly decided that ginger ale was the best thing for that kind of stain. Mrs. Friedman casually positioned herself on the floor and dribbled the soft drink on the afflicted trouser leg. Mother's job was to smile brightly at the Secret Service men as they uncomprehendingly watched the hostess crawling around the president's feet.

If it was entertaining that Lyndon Johnson pretended not to notice that a dog had peed on his leg, another facet of the evening was not so funny. Mother was saddened to see the change in the vice-president's personality in the presence of Numero Uno. Hubert became almost silent after LBJ showed up, and Mother found it painful to see this famously talkative man so silently subservient.

There were occasions in Washington, as elsewhere, when gatherings were not altogether pleasant. A hostile Ann Landers joke was all Mother needed to get her hackles up. She was protective and defensive about the Ann Landers persona, and a slur upon the nature of her work was never ignored. She was particularly infuriated at an embassy reception when the group she was talking with was joied by Senator Eastland. "So you're Ann Landers," he drawled when they were introduced. "Say something funny." Without missing a beat, Mother replied, "Well, you're a politician. Tell me a lie." Everyone's eyes got big, and Senator Eastland quickly excused himself.

Mother's political instincts made her a successful election bettor. She made wagers all over the country on major races. She paid up fast and expected others to do the same. There were times, however, even though she won, when she wasn't entirely pleased with the outcome. Like in 1968 when Mr. Nixon won. Although she had bet he would win, those with whom she had that wager got the following note: "This morning I received your check for $100 — your payment on the election bet. Enclosed is my check for $50. It was a half-assed election."

Chapter 23

The Vietnam war was driving Mother crazy. As a liberal she felt angry and impotent. Whenever there was the chance, she would tell both Lyndon Johnson and Hubert Humphrey that it was the wrong war at the wrong time and that it would ruin both the country and them, as well. Getting nowhere, she decided she had to do *something,* so she arranged a trip in the spring of 1967 to visit our servicemen in the field hospitals.

She was the guest of the Army, with arrangements made by the USO. Hubert was uneasy about her making such a trip. She didn't know, until she came back, that he had requested additional escorts whenever she was in a plane— even General William Westmoreland's own plane, the *White Whale.*

It was a ten-thousand-mile trip and a thirty-three-hour flight from Chicago. She flew to Travis Air Force Base, then

Honolulu, Wake Island, Guam, Manila, and finally Tan Son Nhut Air Base outside Saigon, landing on May 17, the day Cricket was born.

She spent ten days visiting hospitals in Saigon, Qui Nhon, and Camranh Bay. Her trip was reported for the *Sun-Times* by Saul Lockhart and John Donnelly. Their first dispatch pointed out that "Most VIP tourists in Vietnam stick to a schedule, 10–15 minutes a ward, 2–3 hours to a battle zone. Ann Landers visited every bed in every ward, talking to each patient for as long as he cared to or had the strength." She put in twelve-hour days and talked to 2,500 men.

Even in Vietnam Ann Landers was Eppie. She made it a point to wear perfume as well as fatigues. When a young corporal asked her to lean a little closer so he could smell her perfume, she asked, "How long has it been since you've smelled perfume, fella?"

"Ten and a half months," he answered.

"That's all for you, brother. You could be dangerous." She had a personal chat with everyone, bringing the boys up to date about goings-on in the States and chiding the doctors to please get some rest. She could have been anybody's mother, except that she had flown across the world to stroke their foreheads and tell them everything would be all right.

An administrative officer marked that "Most celebrities who come here walk through a couple of wards, get their pictures taken, and leave. This woman has visited every single patient. It's almost eleven at night and I know she's been on her feet since this morning. Where in the world does that little woman get all the energy?"

The closest Hubert came to being right about his fears for

Mother's safety was on Ho Chi Minh's birthday, when she was staying in the home of the commanding general of the Qui Nhon support command. The Viet Cong bombed the backyard, but nothing happened to the house. Mother later mentioned that "some very nice boys" spent the night on the balcony outside her room. The "very nice boys" were MP's who went with her everywhere, although she didn't at first realize that they were assigned to her.

Mother had an appointment to see General Westmoreland, the U.S. commander in chief in Vietnam. She was told beforehand that visits with Westmoreland lasted anywhere from five to twenty-five minutes and that she shouldn't be offended by the devices his staff used to prevent people from staying too long: "You have a phone call, sir," or "Your next appointment is here."

Mother emerged from her visit with "Westy" an hour and twenty mintues after she went in. She was flattered when she noticed that his "phone calls" and "next appointments" were waved away. As the *Sun-Times* report had it, several waiting correspondents wanted to know what the columnist and the general talked about for an hour and twenty minutes.

"Well," said Miss Landers, "the general weighs about 180 pounds. He is just under six feet tall. He does the Royal Canadian Air Force exercises every day and he plays tennis several times a week. He is devoted to his children and is very proud of the hospital work his wife is doing at Clark Air Base in the Philippines."

Did you talk about the war—politics—you know, the pros and cons? "I have nothing to say on that subject," Miss Landers replied emphatically. "Let's leave it at that."

What was her impression of the general? "He's beautiful." She smiled. "I told him that when he retires he ought to go to Hollywood and play generals. He is perfect for the role. But on the serious side, I found him totally committed to his mission—dedicated to his men. And they adore him. He is as tough as a tank and as gentle as a kitten. I wouldn't be surprised if we heard more about this man—in 1972."

The columnist also visited Ambassador Ellsworth Bunker. And what did *they* talk about?

"Mr. Bunker," she commented, "weighs 170 pounds, the same as when he was in college. He is six-feet-plus, and is simply in incredible condition for a man 73 years of age. And he certainly lives up to his reputation for being utterly charming. The ambassador is everything a career diplomat ought to be—and then some."

Mother's version of the Bunker visit was on the level. She felt he was not crazy about the war either, and chose simply to pay her respects. With Westmoreland, on the other hand, she was fired up and vocal on the merits of "the mess." The gist of what she said to him was related in a letter:

This war is immoral, indecent, and unwinnable. It is a disgrace that the United States has become involved in a war 10,000 miles from home against a small poor country . . . a civil war, at that, and one we are going to lose. We are supporting the wrong

side—again—a corrupt clique of crooks and thieves
. . . the Madame Nus and the Diems against the
ragged, poor, starving underdogs. And worse yet,
they are going to kick us out. This war is tearing
our country apart. It does not have the support of
the American people and our campuses are aflame
with protesters.

Her parting shot was more a salvo:

Your generals are bamboozling you. The notion
that all they need is 200,000 more troops is absurd.
We have already poured billions of dollars into that
swamp and are getting our brains beat out. We have
no allies in this war. There are a few troops from
Australia and some from Korea, but all our former
friends have told us they cannot support our
efforts—and they haven't.

(Eleven years later, at Stuart Symington's wedding to Jane
Watson, Mother was on the dance floor when a man in a
gray suit cut in. He said to her with a half-smile, "You
don't remember me, do you?" "No," she 'fessed up, "I'm
sorry I don't." "I'm General Westmoreland," he said, "and
I'll never forget you.")

If some observers of Mother's trip were surprised that a
mere advice columnist was accorded such time and attention in Vietnam, it was probably because they didn't know
that the mere advice columnist then had fifty million daily
readers and political credentials going back to the
Eisenhower administration. She had also been a close friend
of Hubert Humphrey's for almost twenty years.

When Mother returned, she called Ted Hesburgh to

173

check in, report on her trip, and thank him for keeping her alive. Before she had left, he'd told her he would pray for her safety . . . and since she couldn't prove otherwise, she credited him with her well-being. Hence "Andrea Ted."

Mother then phoned the families of all the soldiers she had met who asked her to get in touch with loved ones. As one lieutenant told a reporter in Saigon, "She took down the names and numbers of nearly a hundred men in this hospital alone—and I know she's been to five others."

Mother had recorded pages and pages of people to call— the mothers of GIs everywhere from San Bernardino, California, to Watkins, Minnesota, to Salt Lake City. She had called everyone on her list after four days of phoning and found it one of the most rewarding experiences she'd ever had. The simplest of messages brought boundless joy: "Rick sends you all his love and wants to know how the garden is coming."

Chapter 24

It was probably no accident that I drifted into politics. It was something I had grown up with. My marriage was lousy and I was looking for something to do. I had the time because I had help—or as the children called them years later, "all those crazy-ass maids and butlers."

Nancy Stevenson was a friend, so I volunteered in her husband Adlai III's campaign for state treasurer. I became Nancy's speech writer. This meant that the two of us wrote outlines on the backs of enveloes. Nancy was a first-rate campaigner and the Stevenson name was magic in Illinois. It was particularly helpful that so many small-town residents thought Adlai III was his father or grandfather. Many old-timers cheered us on by saying that Adlai had been a swell vice-president (his grandfather) and a wonderful governor (his father). Whenever I heard that remark, I always thought of the Hoover joke: he had been a serious president, a zealous head of the FBI, and a reliable vacuum cleaner.

Because campaigns didn't go on twelve months a year (at least they didn't then), I had to find other things to do. I tried the pastime of unhappy women everywhere: shop-your-troubles-away. Coleman had the funds, so I became an earnest consumer.

It was, I guess, only a matter of time before I went into analysis. That seemed to be what one did when the bottom fell out—and I knew the bottom had fallen because I was screaming at my husband. The problem was that we were in a restaurant. Mother and Father had asked us to join them at the Pump Room, and I was so wired I just sat there and hollered. The captain was making a Caesar salad. I was making a scene.

The street theater of my discontent was not lost on my mother. She phoned the next morning to say she thought I should make arrangements to see someone. This from the woman who had never wanted me to go to a psychiatrist. "I have already made the call," I told her.

I had, in fact, called Stolar, who through an analyst friend had set me up at the Institute for Psychoanalysis. A doctor would be selected with whom I'd be compatible. Now I didn't have to look around for things to do. I would be going to the shrink four days a week.

The doctor chosen for me was Therese Benedek. I didn't know at the time that she was a well-known specialist for women. All I knew, once I had seen her, was that she was a tiny little old lady in her seventies with an unreconstructed Hungarian accent. She had been in practice so long that she talked with me, and to me, deviating from the classical analytic pattern. The only difficulty was that I didn't always know what she was saying. Early on she told me, "You vant me to give you an Ed Weiss." That was strange, I thought . . . Ed Weiss was Father's advertising man, and even older than Father. I couldn't figure out why she thought he was my problem, or my wish, or my anything. I assured her that she had taken a wrong turn somewhere. "No, no, no," she said impatiently. "You vant me to give you an Ed Weiss . . . like you mother gives Ed Weiss." But of course. Ad-wice.

The thing which most fascinated me in my hours with Dr. Benedek was the work we did on my mother—or, more precisely, Mother and Popo. Their tangled and intertwined relationship apparently had consequences in the next generation. In Mother's quest to be better, to be perfect, she had unwittingly set it up that the less desirable parts of my own personality had no origin. When one's mother is a twin, the resolution is almost unavoidable. In my case, Popo became the "bad" mother in my mind. Rather than accept that my own mother might be flawed and therefore it was all right for me to be, I assigned the unacceptable aspects of my behavior to a person who was not a parent— except that my reflexive instincts could make a case that she was. Popo did, after all, look like my mother, and the two had been subconsciously twisted up in my thinking from the days when I was a small child. When all this had been worked through, $36,000 later, I was better able to accept the strengths and the defects in the trio that was Mother, Popo, and I.

I stayed with Dr. Benedek for four years. We spent a lot of time on my difficulties with Coleman and how I got into them. The analysis ended when I was twenty-nine, along with the marriage, which may have been the point all along.

Mother and Father were wonderfully supportive. They never once said "I told you so." Even though the four newspapers in Chicago steered clear of mentioning my separation and impending divorce—as a courtesy to Mother—my situation was well-known. Mother was determinedly upbeat abut it and took pleasure in closing down "friends" who tried to needle her. People would broach the subject with sympathetic and lowered voices. "How terrible about Margo's divorce." "Oh, no," she would respond, "the divorce is fine. The *marriage* was terrible."

It was widely thought that my divorce changed Mother's mind on the subject. She had, until then, taken the position in her column that couples should stay together, try harder, and work things out. Well-acquainted with my situation, she began to realign her views and look more kindly on ill-suited partners calling it a day. Even Ted Hesburgh shored her up and wished me Godspeed. It meant a great deal to her that a leading Catholic clergyman could see his way clear to saying that divorce was not to be avoided at all costs.

Mother was not unaware of the raised eyebrows caused by Ann Landers' daughter getting a divorce. she was, however, realistic. She had never, from the day she started writing, expected me to regulate my behavior with any thought of how it might reflect on her work.

When I began that new phase of my life, living alone with three children, something happened which was totally unforeseen. I stumbled in a job. Once again, but in a different context, things were back to being Mother, Popo, and I. I wound up in "their" business. And just like Mohter, my journalistic career began by chance.

My firsrt social outing as a solo was the wedding of a chum from Brandeis. My dinner partner was the young cousin of the groom, Gene Siskel. I had known him since he was *nine*. Now he was in his early twenties and the movie critic for the Chicago *Tribune*.

I must never have shut up, because at the end of the evening he told me I was very funny and asked if I wrote. I told him "I don't know" and he said he was going to have someone from his paper call me.

Two days later someone actually did call. A gruff old voice identified himself as Walter Simmons, the *Tribune*'s feature editor, and invited me to come to the paper for a chat. When I showed up I met a white-haired, pink-faced, older gentleman. He didn't horse around with small talk nd his sandpaper voice was in the key of monotone. I adored him from the beginning, probably from the moment he growled that Siskel most likely didn't know his ass from his elbow about spotting writers, but what the hell.

Observing the usual formalities of the business world, I started calling Walter Simnons "Papa Bear." He wanted to know if I'd written anything I could show him. There was one piece, I told him. A year before, I had decided I was George Plimpton and started a book about ten glamorous jobs for women. I outdilettanted Plimpton, however, and did only one jb. I had been a Playboy bunny for three days, and that chapter was in a drawer.

I returned the next day with the typescript and Simmons read it in my presence. He said he wanted to buy it—and that he'd like me to work for him.

My God, an offer of a job. I felt kind of elderly, at twenty-nine, to get into the work force. What did I know about writing, anyway? What did I know about working? My only thought along those lines had been to consider going to law school, but then I thought of my college career and realized it would probably take me eleven years to pass the bar. Not only that, I mentioned the idea to a friend's husband and he told me it sounded tailor-made for me. "You could," he said, "open a law office and boutique."

I decided to take Papa Bear up on his offer. If I had never worked, so what? It would be the better-late-than-never show. Papa Bear said the *Tribune* was ready to take on a younger image, and I would be the youth columnist.

"The youth columnist!" I hooted. "I am going to be thirty."

"That's young around here," he mumbled.

I would be a regular contributor and choose my own subjects. My articles, about 3,000 words, would run, usually on Sundays, two to three weeks apart.

Since I began my apprenticeship on the front page of the feature section, my colleagues knew I was around. Not surprisingly, the saga of Brenda Starr as told to Cinderella did not make me best-beloved newcomer of the year. I never planned it, but my topics usually gave the needle to society pursuits or well-known people. My efforts earned me a new name: That Bitch.

As if it weren't enough that I was Papa Bear's protégée, my lack of experience was well known. It was also known that I drove to work in a Rolls-Royce and lived in a seventeen-room apartment. I had as many servants as children, and of course there were Mother and Father, not exactly a low-profile couple in Chicago.

There was, naturally, speculation that I had shacked up with someone in the composing room, that I had something on Papa Bear, or that Mother "bought" the job for me. These well-wishers didn't make much of a dent in my spirit because the newspaper business is one of the few enterprises in which the performance is so public that it doesn't matter whose kid you are, or whose girlfriend. More important, the *Tribune* wasn't Mother's paper, it was the competition.

When my work started to attract attention, the *Sun-Times* was frantic. Why was I not with them? Mother was loving it. She told them with great glee that I had offered them the bunny piece but their feature editor didn't like it.

Of course I had no field, so they called my stuff "social commentary." To my amazement, my one or two pieces a month were prompting people to write or call the *Trib* to ask why I wasn't writing more often. Papa Bear made his move. He called me in and offered me a thrice-weekly column.

"Make it two, and you're on," I countered. My byline became simply "Margo." My first column was about dancing for disease, all those parties to benefit heart defects, deafness, cancer, and rheumatism. Papa Bear, of course, was always running interference for me. He later said, somewhat wistfully, "You are the star in my crown and the thorn in my side."

After I had written the column for six months, Papa Bear advised me that the Chicago *Tribune*/New York *Daily News* syndicate wanted to talk. They were sending someone to Chicago.

I was horrified. It was one thing to have gotten lucky in

my home town, but I wasn't convinced I would have any success laying my views on the rest of America. I told Papa Bear I had serious reservations. He was encouraging. "You're young," he said, "and you're different. I think you could be very big." Sure, I thought, If God drops everything else.

What the *Tribune/Daily News* syndicate sent to Chicago instead of a representative was a message: they had to bow out because their star, "Dear Abby," did not want me in the same syndicate.

When word got around that I was dead at that syndicate, two others wanted to talk. One of them had been in business for about five minutes and Papa Bear elected to pass. The other one was considered the best in the business, owned by Marshall Field—and their star was Ann Landers. Papa Bear speculated that this was their way of luring me away from the *Tribune,* but it would be worth it, he said, because "Syndication is what this business is about."

I did not want to leave him and I did not want to leave a paper that took me from nowhere and allowed me to build a name. The *Tribune* was a generous employer. Leaving was not my idea of how to say thank you. Papa Bear, who would soon be fighting his own battles at the *Tribune,* told me he would be retiring in a little over a year and that he wanted me to go.

There was one other person I needed the go-ahead from. My mother. If Popo didn't want me in her syndicate, then maybe I would pose a problem for Mother, as well. Her answer was that I should come ahead. And she sent me a welcome gift: a big electric typewriter like the one she used.

*   *   *

If I had been entertaining myself while at the *Tribune,* being syndicated was like running a business. There was even a sales force to sell features, and the salesmen all seemed partial to comic strips. Text columns were not nearly so easy to sell. I remember the day the chief salesman told me he admired my spunk but didn't undeerstand a word I wrote. He graciously added, though, that he would do his best to get me into some good papers. My only concern was that I didn't like the way he knocked wood when he said it.

The "Margo" column was, indeed, bought by good papers: the Baltimore *Sun,* the Detroit *News,* the Philadelphia *Bulletin,* the Los Angeles *Times,* and the Washington *Post.* I was to learn the vagaries of the syndicate business as I went. The Washington *Post*, for example, bought my column but never ran it. This, I was told, was so the Washington *Star* couldn't have it. Mother said she had experienced the same thing in Philadelphia. I was also bounced out of te Boston *Globe* when my home paper, the Chicago *Daily News,* canceled the wife of the *Globe*'s editor. She wrote an advice column called "Dear Beth."

Erma Bombeck, when she lived in Dayton, generously sent me a package of all the promotion when the Dayton *Journal Herald* bought my column. "You are," she wrote me, "the queen of Dayton." Six months later I found out which queen I was. Marie Antoinette. They decided to ax the column.

I added papers, I lost papers, and my little lark had turned into a business. I was earning $50,000 a year shooting off my mouth, and the whole thing seemed a little odd. I will never forget walking into the syndicate office and learning that David Lawrence, a columnist in his eighties, had died. A promotion man was beside himself. "My God," he wailed, "imagine dying right before a sales meeting!" Thoughtless of him, I agreed, and wondered how I had gotten into such a business.

Chapter 25

M other, however, felt right at home. She was totally comfortable in the newspaper world, and much of her life was filtered through it. When she said, "Let me tell you about my operation," she was talking about her office. Her secretaries—as many as thirteen at one time—have always been her "girls." There have been many over the years. Some came to her imagining they would end up writing the column, others signed on because their own lives were troubled and they thought if they could just get close to her all would be well. A few of the "girls" were competitive with me, becoming fantasy sisters vying for the attenion of "our" mother. Many were quite good friends, and one or two were just plain nuts.

God forbid working for Ann Landers should be all work and no education; Mother scheduled periodic sessions in the office which she called "philosophies." She would snare a friend, sometimes famous, to come and give the "girls" something new to think about. Mother thought that information from diverse sources was important for her staff because some of them answered reader mail that didn't get into the paper, and she wanted them to operate on their own whenever it was possible. Often, people simply needed a referral to a pubic agency. And some problems, of course, came in thousands of times—almost word for word—and for these there were form letters. The advice is not going to vary too much when the plaint is from a young girl who writes, "I absolutely can't stand my legs and my mother won't let me shave them." To these petitioners went what Mother called "the hairy-leg form." Her advice was,"Shave."

There was always nut mail, which Mother and the "Girls" became adept at spotting quickly. Three mentions of Jesus in the first sentence gave them the clue, as did repeated use of "the S. word" and "the F. word." Even these letters, if they had names and addresses, were answered. Mother would scrawl her own acronym at the bottom of such missives, telling the secretaries that the response was to be GLATFW,"the spoken version of which was "Glatva." That meant "good luck and thanks for writing."

People who wrote to Ann Landers were not always looking for advice. Sometimes they would dream up scenarios of misery to see if they could trick Ann Landers into falling for a made-up problem. This endeavor has become a kind of pop journalistic work of art. People would also write to her when they wanted to go beyond the professional relationship. Once in a while these letters involved me. My favorite was sent while I was at Brandeis.

A fellow from Harvard went on at great length about "a rudeness" he was subjected to by a young lady: he had merely called her for a coffee date and then had to listen to a five-minute "harangue" about why, of course, she wasn't going.

Mother responded that such rudeness was unforgivable. Her answer was then mailed *back* to her with a note that her daughter had been the young lady and what did she think now? She responded again:

> Any young man who would take the trouble to write me, as you did, in the hope of getting a young lady in dutch, must be a jerk. I am sure she did the right thing by refusing the date.

Although she made a conscious effort not to become involved with readers' problems, there were times when her gut overrode her judgment. There was a young woman in Ohio, for example, who touched some chord as they corresponded for months. Finally Mother recommended psychiatric help for her . . . and paid for it. And every now and then she would agree to meet with a reader if she felt a face-to-face encounter would accomplish something important. Her social friends, of course, decided that she had magic solutions and began to tell her all manner of personal problems. I don't think she at all minded being on the inside. Her insiderhood, however, produced one unattractive side effect: it became hard for her to resist playing a sophisticated version of the kids' game, "I know something you don't know." She would toy around with hints, although being maddeningly careful never to spill the beans. I found it insanely provocative to hear that I wouldn't believe the mess the Clarks were in, but of course she could say no more.

Her ego, on occasion, would put her in a no-win situation. She assumed that from the sheer strength of her experience and clear thinking she could straighten out anything, at least when mediating between friends. Whenever she failed, she was truly surprised. Having "clout," as they say in Chicago—and she had it in great abundance—made any area of ineffectiveness difficult for her to comprehend. The name alone, "Ann Landers," came to signify authority and correctness. The name was powerful because it meant something, and it stood for something. A brand of toothpaste offered her a million dollars for a series of print ads—and this was in the 1960's. A sewing machine company wanted a single endorsement for which they were willing to pay $100,000. Advertising people were not the only ones with the hope of tying her name to a product. The Chicago Democratic machine put out a feeler: would she be interested in running against Everett Dirksen? She never, of course, did any of these things, understanding that it wouldn't be fair to use the name in a way that God, and her publisher, had not intended.

I was perhaps among the last to catch on to her importance. I think any child would be, unless the family surname were Perón or Pahlavi. Mother knew I didn't get it, and my lack of deference was a running joke between us. In November 1978, she sent me a wire-service story naming her "Most influential woman in America" according to *The World Almanac*'s fourth annual selection. Her note with the clipping was brief: *"Now* will you listen to me? L & K, Nanno."

*   *   *

I called Mother Nanno, probably because the children did.Father called her "the Queen." He also called her Pollyana, believing her to be incredibly naive at times. One of those times was during the Linda Lovelace *Deep Throat* hype. Reading that Lovelace was scheduled to tape *Kup's Show* in Chicago, Mother called Kup—Essie Kupcinet—to ask if she could join the panel—just to make sure there was someone to stick up for propriety. Of course Kup was thrilled. Ann Landers and Linda Lovelace was some parley. The taping was even rescheduled to accommodate Mother.

Then she called me because she knew I had seen the movie and interviewed Ms. Lovelace for my column. "It's a trashy movie, isn't it?" she asked. Well yes, I said, but it made me laugh.

"But she's not actually undressed or anything, is she?" Mother queried.

"Undressed!" I shrieked. "Most of the time she is stark naked."

There was a long pause. "You don't mean you can see her hermans!" ("Hermans" being a family word for "bosom.")

"Hers and everybody else's. Listen, you don't know much about this movie, do you?"

Well, no, she didn't. She just understood it was a little racy.

"What do you think 'deep throat' means?" I asked.

"I haven't the faintest idea," she told me.

I explained it. There was an even longer pause this time.

"I will get myself off the show."

"But you went out of your way to get yourself on. They even rescheduled the taping. How can you bow out?"

"I suppose I can't," she whispered. And then, not quite

believing the whole thing, she had a final question. "You can really see her hermans?"

She must never see this movie, I thought. She would have cardiac arrest and burn down the theater while waiting for the ambulance.

I knew *Kup's Show* would be wonderful, but I didn't know how wonderful. The afternoon of the taping, I had a luncheon interview with Niven Busch, the screenwriter who had written *Duel in the Sun*. He asked if I'd like to tag along while he did the second segment of *Kup's Show*. Of course I said yes. That meant I could watch the first segment.

When we got to the studio, I waved to Mother and sat down with Busch. It wasn't an audience show, but there was a handful of people—publicists, agents, families of guests.

They rolled the tape. Kup introduced the panel: Mother, Ms. Lovelace, Joel Grey and Drew Middleton from the *New York Times*. Mother asked if she could make a short explanatory statement. She looked right into the camera and launched into a graphic and medically correct definition of the phrase "deep throat," just in case those at home were ignorant of it—as she had been.

They went crazy in the control room. The engineer was waving his arms, the producer slapped both hands over his mouth, Irv Kupcinet was holding his forehead. There was a quick decision to keep going. It was a late-night show and they would take their chances getting the opening minutes on the air.

They made it. When the show aired, I heard from dozens of people that a healthy percentage of Chicago was phoning up friends to get them to watch. What they saw was

Lovelace defending her "art," Mother talking about love and decency, and Joel Grey choosing up sides with Ms. Lovelace.

Mother said at one point that movies like *Deep Throat* were no different from watching dogs do it in the street. Joel Grey then asked how she knew those dogs weren't in love. Mother later told me she couldn't understand why Joel Grey might want to curry favor with Miss Lovelace, but that it was certainly his prerogative.

Chapter 26

Mother liked being a celebrity. She was never bored or bothered by attention from strangers. They were, after all, her people—the ones who wrote to find answers, or to bitch, or to say thank you. Whether people saw her or heard her voice, they instinctively came over. For most of them she was less a famous face than an old friend—albeit one they'd never met before.

Mother didn't always know who other celebrities were, however. Once, when introduced to Peter, Paul, and Mary, she told the group: "What darling names—all from the Bible." She had no idea who they were or what they did. She would have recognized Erroll Garner, maybe, or Frank Sinatra, but that's about it. I was sympathetic to such gaps in her knowledge, having once myself asked a man named Sam Snead what he did for a living.

While Mother's ignorance of many theatrical people was

genuine, I think it was also willed—that she chose not to know too much about performers because, long ago, she had known too much. Going all the way back to A.B.'s theaters was the little girl's remembrance of singers, comics, and chorus girls. Mother perhaps felt one thing and thought another. The issue is an old one: to be drawn to something emotionally but to decide intellectually that it is unimportant . . . a little like forsaking the circus to be an MD. The irony is that Mother's manner is theatrical. She makes entrances and exits, attracts attention wherever she goes, and in the company of others is in control. She is hardly ever seen in public without makeup and a stylish outfit—an entertainer herself in the sense that she, too, has a public. It is for them, perhaps, that television appearances and formal affairs find her in red knit, black beads, or white fringe.

Mother's preference for politicians over performers cannot be wholly unrelated to Popo's interest in show biz. The days of their youth, when they shared the same friends, are long gone.

Most of Mother's friends were men, not because she preferred them to women but because they were the movers and shakers in the areas she cared about. There were always, and there are now, more men than women in politics, newspapers, and the medical establishment. Father was never jealous, and indeed I don't think there was anything to be jealous of.

When I reached an age when it was germaine, Mother told me her view of operating in a world of men. When you received an "offer," which was her word for "proposition,"

194

the trick was to say no in such a way that the gentleman didn't feel like a jerk. There is no reason for total destruction, she theorized. I liked her for not making the whole thing a question of morality. She simply felt if a woman engaged in a romance here and there that when the romance was over, the relationship would be, too. It was that simple as far as she was concerned: one's access would become limited. The question for her was fling versus friendship.

She also had a way to manage with jealous wives: just concentrate on *them*—"defang them" is how she put it. "Once you make it plain that your interest is not centered around their husbands, they are friends for life."

If some of Mother's concepts were formulated with cold-eyed calculation, others evolved from naiveté. Her approach to religion, for example, was simplistic and childlike. It was because of her that for years I thought of God as a supernatural cop. I even adopted her perception that He was a kindly giant of a man with white hair and a beard who sat on a sturdy chair, slightly resembling a throne, who somehow knew what everybody was doing.

Mother didn't know one Jewish holiday from another, with the exception of Chanukah and the high holy days, but she felt religious. Friday-night candles were always lit when she was home, although the accompanying Hebrew prayer never came out the same way twice. Like many Reformed Jews, Mother made it a point to attend temple for Rosh Hashanah and Yom Kippur services, until she decided that the rabbis were uninspiring and maybe she didn't have to go. She probably knew a great deal more about Catholicism than Judaism.

In speaking of her faith to Eugene Kennedy for his book *Believing,* she made no effort to make her beliefs sound more grown-up.

"I believe in a good God," she said. "Incidentally, my belief in God is somewhat infantile. I think He is loving and all-protecting because he has loved and protected me. This is a very personal thing. I talk to him all the time, like Tevye in *Fiddler on the Roof.* I call God up like I call anybody up, and his line is never busy."

The little girl in her found other ways to come out. In an interview in which she talked about her support for Gene McCarthy, she managed to call him "goofy." And speaking of Hubert Humphrey to a reporter, she made the following observation: "That man has an incredible capacity to bounce back into life. The trouble is people sometimes get the wrong idea about Hubert. They talk about 'Hubert the joke' or 'Hubert the potato head,' and he is not that way at all."

Now, most people, when speaking for attribution, would not refer to a friend as 'goofy' or "a potato head," and I would be one of them. But that was part of Mother's one-of-a-kind-ness— either not knowing or not caring how a remark would play. If she had something to say, she said it, which made her by no means smooth in the classical sense.

Smooth or not, she was gutsy. "Principles," I guess, is the word. *Oh, Mother, you're so principalic.* She never seemed afraid to go out on a limb, even when there was the chance the limb might break. There was one dance of danger that I loved her for, although I didn't think she was right. It was when the Justice Department, through the U.S. attorney's office in Chicago, was trying to hang a drug rap on Hugh Hefner and some of his people. Although Hef had for years been trying to engage Mother in a public dialogue—the Puritan and the Playboy, as it were—she continually declined . . . but she liked him and they were friends. When the investigation heated up, Mother made Hef an offer: if he wound up in a trial, she would appear as a character witness. There never was a trial, but the offer was genuine. Dick Rosenzweig, who worked for *Playboy,* said that Eppie and Hef's own parents were the only people, who, when they dined at the mansion in Chicago, inspired Hef to wear a suit instead of a bathrobe. Although the age difference wasn't quite right, I felt Hef regarded her as a mother.

There were other times when Mother's social conscience was simply that: social. I remember when she purposefully invited Otto Kerner to her parties after he had been indicted. She wanted to show solidarity with an old friend, and that was the best way she could think of. Her reasoning was that she had included him when he was governor, so why cut him off when he had trouble.

Class, as well as friendship, was a concept that was always rattling around in her head. It meant doing the right thing and trying to be better. Her ideas on the subject found their way into print some years ago:

Dear Ann Landers:
What is class? John F. Kennedy had it. Other presidents have had it, too, but with JFK it just stuck out all over.

Bernard Baruch has it. Paul Getty doesn't. Grace Kelly and Deborah Kerr have it. Jayne Mansfield and Mamie Van Doren—no. King Gustav of Sweden has it but not so King Farouk. Prince Phillip, yes. His brother-in-law, no.

Warren Spahn has it, but Bo Belinsky doesn't. Perry Como has it in abundance—Liberace not a trace. Gary Cooper—yup. John Wayne, nope.

We talk about people who have class, yet no one seems to know what it is. What is class anyway?

EPB

Dear EPB:

Class is an aura of confidence that comes with knowing you've got the goods. It's being sure without being cocky.

Jacob had it, Esau didn't. Symbolically we can look to Jacob's wrestling with the angel. Those with class have wrestled with the angel. Those with class have wrestled with their particular angel and won a victory that marks them thereafter.

Class has nothing to do with money. The wealthiest man in town can be notably without class, while the cop on the beat can ooze class from every pore.

Class never runs scared. Class is self-discipline and self-knowledge; it's the surefootedness that comes with having proved that you can meet life and beat it to the draw.

She meant every word of it, too, although I'm not sure how she squared away JFK's peccadilloes with really classy behavior. Perhaps she thought that part of his personality

was outweighed by his other qualities. Her plea was always
for understanding. I greatly admired her ability to forgive,
a quality which, in me, measured about zero. An example
of this difference between us was evident when Hubert was
in his last illness. I wrote him a letter and sent it to his
apartment, knowing he would be deluged with mail at the
office. When I got a printed reply card, I made a snide
remark to Mother about how glad I was that I had written.
She responded with a note . . . with enclosures, of course:

Dear Margo,
   If you didn't like your thank-you from Hubert,
get a load of this!
   There followed a Xerox copy of a note from
Hubert:
Dear Eppie,
   Thank you for the beautiful floral arrangement you
sent me in the hospital. It brought cheer to both
Muriel and me during a very difficult time. Best of
all, however, was just to be remembered by you.
   Then there was a copy of her response to that
letter:
Dear Hubert,
   Thank you for Form Letter 27, a copy of which is
hereby enclosed. I did not send "a beautiful floral
arrangement." I sent two custom-made ties, for
which you thanked me profusely by letter, phone,
and in person.
   I don't envy you the job of responding to all who
sent "beautiful floral arrangements"—and books,
letters, cards, telegrams, and prayers. I'll bet you've
got 10,000 letters ahead of you—and Christmas is

breathing down your neck! Always at this time of year I'm so glad I'm Jewish. I can ignore all that holly-wreath and ho-ho-ho stuff—and stick strictly with Chanukah, which is no big deal.

Her note to me continued:

You must bear in mind that Hubert received at least 10,000 messages, gifts, bouquets, notes, etc., etc., etc. I don't have to tell you about his staff. What surprises me is that anybody got any kind of
thank-you. L & K,
Nanno

Chapter 27

Every once in a while Mother talked about personal things in the column. She would mention her age, or religion, some past experience—even me—if she thought such information would help make a point. On rare occasions she devoted the entire column to a personal reminiscence. The first time was when she wrote about my grandmother Gustie as the world's best mother-in-law. The second time was when she and Father celebrated their thirtieth anniversary.

Dear Readers:
This may be just another day to you, but it is a very special day in my life. Thirty years ago, on a sweltering Sunday afternoon in Sioux City, Iowa, Jules Lederer slipped a plain gold band on my finger and I became his wife.

Honesty forbids me describing myself as a student at Morningside College, so I'll simply say I was enrolled there. Jules had had one year at Northwestern—High School, that is. He was a product of Detroit, handsome, energetic, imaginative, a born optimist and eager to take on the world. He had a good job and a promising future. He was also broke.

I was an effervescent, fun-loving girl, hopelessly square, driven by a crusading spirit to save the world—sort of a Jewish Joan of Arc. I was also engaged to marry a law student in California. But Jules, never one to be discouraged by small obstacles, asked me to marry him anyway. I said yes, and the wedding took place three months later.

We were blessed the following year with a baby girl, Margo. From then on, I saw more of the moving van than I saw of Jules. When an opportunity for advancement arose, he took it. And it seemed always to be in another city.

We moved from Sioux City to St. Louis, from St. Louis to New Orleans, from New Orleans to Milwaukee. Then came World War II and Jules served in the infantry. In 1945 we moved from Little Rock to Los Angeles, from Los Angeles to Eau Claire, Wisconsin, and from Eau Claire to Chicago.

Time, that subtle thief of youth, is often cursed by those who long to stop the clock, or turn it back, but we want none of that. Each year has been better than the last because we have grown together. A good marriage, it is said, is made in heaven. This might be true, but the maintenance work must be

done right down here. A successful marriage is not a
gift, it is an achievement. No real marriage can exist
without differences in opinion and the ensuing
battles. But battles can be healthy. They bring to
marriage the vital principle of equal partnership. If
there is a secret to making marriage work it is
"Never go to bed mad."

Our thirty years together have been blessed with
good health, good fortune, good friends, good times,
and success. Jules says he could not have made it
without me. I am not sure he is right. But I could
not have made it without him, and of *this* I am
certain. He taught me how to be alone without
feeling sorry for myself. He taught me never to back
away from a challenge—that it is better to try and
fail and then to try again. He taught me how to use
my time productively. His work habits are
impeccable. I learned mine from him.

Being Mrs. Jules Lederer has been superb training
for Ann Landers. Thirty years with this unselfish,
supportive, responsive man has enabled me to live life
as few people have the opportunity to live it. Being
Ann Landers' husband could pose a terrible problem,
but Jules has met the challenge with dignity and
incredible good humor. My husband is my best friend
and I am his. I consider it a privilege to be the wife of
this beautiful guy who took on the world with a tenth-
grade education and a hole in his sock.

Father's socks no longer had holes in them, but they
were still in shoes that ran for planes. There was no such
thing as slowing down; work at half-tilt would be boring.

After thirty years Mother knew that her suggestion, as a bride, for the Lederer family crest had been apt: bagels and lox and a pickax. All the effort, of course, paid off. Father had built a big business and everybody knew it.

Among his admirers, in the late 1960's, were the conglomerate inhalers of hot companies. They not only respected Budget, they wanted to buy it. Father knew he shouldn't sell—it would be tantamount to giving up his baby. Every one of his friends who had been bought out later regretted it. "You get a lot of money or stock," they told him, "but the business is never run right and they ignore you in the bargain. Once the management contract runs out, you're given a warm handshake and a good-bye." Guys with little buy-outs, five million dollars, or big ones, one hundred million, all counseled him to ignore the offers and own his own business.

Father listened to all the advice and then sold Budget to Transamerica. It was just too tempting to be given ten million dollars for a nine-year-old company. He rationalized that he would lie back a little, then build something new.

The sale was effected in stock, not cash. That way Father could avoid the taxes and also make a fate bet: he was gambling that the price of the stock would go up. Father thanked the people who worked for him in a way that seemed appropriate. He took one million dollars of his share and gave it to them.

In 1972, three years after the sale to Transamerica, Father was a mogul emeritus and Mother felt he should live like one. She bought a palatial old apartment a block from where they were. It was fourteen rooms of magnificent paneling, splendid woods, and elegant appointments. Father called it "the bowling alley."

With this apartment Mother changed her whole style. She not only switched from boxy-modern to spacious-grand, her taste underwent a complete metamorphosis. The old fondness for vivid reds and greens gave way to a yen for pastels. Now her colors were apricot and cream, accented with English antiques and a touch of chinoiserie. For the first time, she engaged a decorator and thought about serious art. Father encouraged her by giving her the Salvador Dali bronze head of John Kennedy. It was from an edition of six, one of which was in the Kennedy Center in Washington. Then Father had buyer's remorse, feeling that he had been ripped off. "I think I made a mistake," he told me, "paying $25,000 for something that's not even an original." I explained about castings, and he seemed reassured.

That was not, however, the last question about the Dali. Many weeks later, Mother called with a problem. One of the help had knocked an ear off while dusting and was obviously afraid to tell her. She wasn't going to fire anybody, but she did want the ear back. Could I come over and help her figure out what to do?

I arrived and went to inspect the damage. The place where she thought the ear had been was perfectly smooth and finished—no one had knocked off anything. Mother was just not used to renderings that weren't totally realistic and apparently never noticed "the missing ear" before. Pointing out the smoothness of the area and the patina, which matched the rest of the bronze, I explained that this was by Dali, after all, and she was lucky the face had a nose. Relieved, she told me how impressed she was with

205

my knowledge of art. I said almost anyone could have helped her out. This, however, she chalked up to modesty. Mothers are like that.

That Father bought a Dali in the first place was no great surprise. His approach to money was consistent (always generous) whereas Mother would swerve back and forth. Her financial behavior was not predictable. She would make bounteous gifts to charitable appeals; she would also bring home sugar packets from airplanes and reuse Saran wrap. This last frugality is harder than it sounds. You have to unwrap a bowl gingerly, keeping the electrically charged cellophane intact, then wash it, dry it, and put it away.

Economy one day could be followed by largesse the next. An example: Mother's gifts to me, for the most part, were modest mementos. A little before my thirty-first birthday I was carrying on about the asymmetry of the number thirty-one. It seemed a horrible age to have to say you were. Thirty was fine, thirty-two would be good, but thirty-one? Mother's gift to me for that odd-numbered birthday was a white mink coat with black markings—like one of hers that I admired. She wanted to cheer me up and surprise me . . . both of which can be done very well with a mink coat.

I am sure it was the way I was raised, rather than some hard-and-fast rule of modern life, which suggested to me that a mink coat from your mother means maybe it's time to have a husband. From the time of my separation from Coleman I had dated marvelous men who were stimulating and accomplished. The idea of trying it again didn't seem particularly out of the question. It is true that remarriage is the triumph of hope over experience, so it was with a feeling of optimism that I did something that seemed terribly sensible: I decided to marry an undertaker whose hobby was refereeing hockey games. I thought I should be with someone settled, someone real. My second husband was Jules Furth.

Mother and Father were not frantic this time about my choice. They were somewhere between neutral and approving, and they thought he was a sweet guy, as did almost everybody. Mother could not resist one small remark, however. "Did you search the world," she asked, "for someone with your father's name?"

Chapter 28

The "original" Jules was now fighting the Boer Wars, and the Boers were his partners, the conglomerate. The arrangement with Transamerica was going just as his friends had predicted. Badly. Father was in the middle of a five-year management contract that was breaking his heart. The brass at Trans were paying him a salary; they were not, however, listening to him. The feeling of betrayal and frustration was exacerbated by the fact that if they had put him out to pasture, he had sold them the land.

Mother, as always, was optimistic. She reassured Father he would land on his feet — the same thing she had told him when he picked up and left Presto. He was so dispirited, however, that her hopefulness was an irritant.

She said things would be fine.

He was not so sure.

In the beginning, when he made the deal, Father

thought he would wind up as chairman of Trans. Now he knew at the end of five years he would be removed from Budget.

He had started to invest. With Victor Lownes, a partner of Hugh Hefner's, he bought the Great American Disaster, a trendy hamburger joint in London. He started a business which imported English nurses to American hospitals, then a computer firm that billed insurance companies. And God only knows why, he bought a company in Switzerland that manufactured signs from broken-bottle pieces.

As he was fond of saying, "When the dice are cold, they're all cold." His investments were not turning out well. Europe became a palliative place . . . it was "older," it was more "civilized." Already having major business interests in London, Father bought a mews housse near Hyde Park. Maybe an ocean would put distance between him and the mistake of selling Budget.

When he began having difficulties with some of the people he had associated himself with, Mother urged him to undo these relationships. He felt he couldn't, so he stuck around to battle it out with lawsuits. His business life was severely troubled but it was the only life he had. When he was home, lawyers and bankers were his companions during the day. Double Scotches kept him company at night. There were midnight calls to Transamerica executives telling them they were shmucks. Not only weren't they listening to him, they were presiding over the one thing Father had never expected: the price of their stock went down. From 42 to 9, to be precise.

Whereas, for years, the pattern had been for Mother and Father to pursue their careers with a shared sense of joy, now things had changed. He was fractionated and over-wrought; his formerly beloved business life had become a struggle with new problems every day. He responded by distancing himself from Mother. Maybe he was embarrassed, maybe he was sparing her his depression. Maybe maybe. People never tell you why they're doing what they're doing. Often they themselves don't know.

One can only listen so much and talk so much until there is a need to shield oneself from someone else's pain. For Mother, the haven was her work. If she couldn't help her chum of more than thirty years, she would at least keep her own life going.

An irony of their situation was that while Father was deliberately not taking care of himself, Mother was much concerned with health. Her work had, in fact, allowed her to gain entry to a world which had always fascinated her. Medicine. Her ticket of admission was the name Ann Landers and her contribution was the influence attached to the name.

Short of seeing patients, she was playing Doctor in a big way: as a member of the Visiting Committee for the Board of Overseers for Harvard Medical School, on the Mayo Clinic's Sponsors Committee, and as a trustee of Meharry Medical College, the Menninger Foundation, and the Deree-Pierce College in Greece. She served also on the national boards of the American Cancer Society, the National Dermatology Foundation, the Rehabilitation Institute of Chicago, and the Hereditary Disease Foundation. There was a presidential appointment in 1979 to the Advisory Board of the National Cancer Institute.

Her interest in medicine, I suspect, had to do with the death of her parents at a relatively young age, a concern for her own health, information she had gleaned from spending time with Stolar, and the traditional Jewish reverence for "my son, the doctor." That Ann Landers sometimes functioned as a mail-order diagnostician merely legitimated her interest.

It could not have been a coincidence that her dearest friend of later years was Mary Lasker, the New Yorker who presides over the Lasker Award for Medicine. The two of them knew every drug around and whether or not they thought it had possibilities!

Mother's identification with things medical got her invited on the first AMA trip to China, shortly after the government permitted Americans to travel there again. She was the only nonphysician in the AMA group of sixteen.

She went in September 1974, and wrote a week's worth of columns on her China experience, a mini-version of her reporting from Russia. While her observations were colorful, I felt they missed the boat entirely. She chose to concentrate on how clean, well-behaved, and polite the people were, totally glossing over the repressive nature of the society. It was more important to her that schoolchildren greeted visitors by saying in unison, "Good morning, American aunties and uncles," than the fact that handholding was outlawed in public.

She had, however, solved her problem of fifteen years earlier in Russia, when she didn't know what to do about making toasts to friendship. Whereas then she downed a shot of vodka, neat, now she played the game with orange soda. As she told her readers, she felt she had lucked out: a doctor from Indianapolis described the mai-tais as "rocket fuel."

While an entire column was devoted to Dr. George

Hatem, the American physician who eradicated VD in China, the political structure was hardly discussed. As close as she came was this paragraph from her last dispatch:

In two decades China has defeated malnutrition, plague, cholera, typhoid fever, VD, drug addiction, alcoholism, and crime. There are virtually no bullet- or knife-wound patients to treat. Life, for the masses, is infinitely better. Still, not everyone loves the People's Republic. At least 300 a month risk their lives trying to escape by swimming to Hong Kong via Deep, or Mirs, Bay.

When she returned home I told her, when she asked, that from my admittedly more radical position I felt she had been soft in her analysis. She said perhaps, yes, but she had a recollection of Chiang Kai-shek which I did not.

There was one thing, however, she did in those China columns that I would have done. It had to do with gossip.

I learned something about minding my own busiess, which seems to be an old Chinese custom. I made several inquiries about Chairman Mao's wife. "Is she his third or fourth?" I asked. (Actually, she's his third.) No one could tell me a single thing about Mao's previous marriages.

When I tried to pump a woman I knew to be extremely knowledgeable, I was put in my place. "The Chinese are not interested in the sex lives of their public figures," she replied crisply. "Unlike Americans, they don't discuss the private affairs of their leaders."

213

*   *   *

A bittersweet footnote to all of Mother's medical involvement had to do with an old friend, the fellow she had been engaged to before Father. They had always stayed in touch, and when he developed kidney disease as a middle-aged man, he and his wife, Beth, asked Mother to help them arrange treatment. Since there were waiting lists for kidney patients everywhere, Mother intervened with the nephrology department at Harvard. Lewis Dreyer was accepted at a Boston hospital for a transplant. When he finally died, more than five years later, Beth Dreyer wrote Mother about how much those five years had meant. Mother remarked, when she got the letter, that it caused her to ponder five years as a block of time . . . it could seem either like a flash or very long, indeed.

Chapter 29

For me, five years marked the span of my newspaper career. I retired the column called "Margo" to resume a life of home, hearth, and Bonwit's. Never having been terribly motivated in the first place, I was pleased to have done *something,* but a three-a-week syndicated feature was clearly no part-time job. I felt the impact of my decision when I was introduced at a party as the girl who "used to be" Margo.

Mother's reaction to her daughter, the has-been, was that of a friend. Whatever I felt was best for me was the thing to do. She had loved the compliments on my work and now she would be proud of me for choosing to be a housewife. She never confused my drive with hers.

It was a fall night in 1974. It was raining. Of course it would have been raining. When Jules Furth and I had finished dinner, Father phoned and asked if he could drop by. When he showed up, Furth and I took our coffee into the little yellow sitting room off the master bedroom. It was the coziest place to be in that mammoth apartment, all yellow and filled with my favorite things. A fire was going in the silly ornate fireplace which seemed to cancel out the rain on the other side of the heavy draperies. Would Father like some coffee? Actually, he'd prefer a Scotch.

Then, in a flow of rain and Scotch, I was part of the saddest conversation I could remember. Father had come to tell me he was in love with an Englishwoman. What he was really doing, however, was asking my permission to divorce Eppie. The way he put it was: Would you still see me if I divorced your mother?"

I was absolutely flabbergasted. Such a possibility had never crossed my mind. In fact, I thought he was perfect, never mind seeing other women. I knew he was having business troubles but I had not known he had woven them to include Mother. What would he do when he got divorced? I asked. He planned to marry Elizabeth, came the answer. Elizabeth. My head was spinning and an uncomfortable ball became a part of my throat. It was hard to swallow, so it was hard to speak. "Who is Elizabeth, exactly? I managed. Well, Elizabeth is a nurse. Father elaborated that the situation was complicated because she was six years my junior. The lady was 28 years old, Father was 56.

Perhaps these plans were a hasty idea about how to change his life and change his luck, I suggested. How long had Elizabeth been around? I asked. The answer just tightened the ball in my throat. Three years.

Did Elizabeth still live in London? By then I almost didn't need to ask. Not only did she live in London, she lived in Father's Mews house, the one he and Mother had bought.

Now I understood the meaning of a lunch we had had months earlier. Father and I had met at a deli and he steered the conversation to all of Mother's famous friends. Why did she have them? Why did she care so much? Wasn't there anybody around worth liking who wasn't an overachiever?

I told him I had thought some of those thoughts myself. He seemed comforted. The only difference between my resolution and his, however, was that I finally figured it out, and he never did. It became clear to me, as I thought about it, that people who were accomplished were fun. Mother herself was well-known, and famous people tended to see other famous people. And, to be totally accurate, not all her friends were prominent. The famous-friend argument had become one of Father's justifications for deciding there was something wrong with with his wife.

There followed, in that night of awful surprises, a recital by Father of Mother's shortcomings. His complaints were mean-spirited and irrational. When he got to his grievance about how she had always belittled him for being too short for the Air Force, I thought, for the first time that night, he might not be well. He sure as hell wasn't sober.

Properly motivated or not, Father clearly hadn't made Elizabeth up, and he seemed determined to redo his life. Which brought us back to his reason for coming over: would I still see him if he divorced my mother.? I said I would; that everybody got to make his own moves. After all, I was remarried.

I was trying to analyze things and trying to think. What I was doing best, however, was listening to the rain. I had always loved the rain. Now I wasn't so sure. I tried to retreat to a time of greater safety, and my disjointed abstractions took me back to when I was a little girl. I couldn't stay there long, however. Father walked over to my chair with a snapshot of Elizabeth. "Very attractive," I said, while thinking: well, he said she was a nurse, not a movie star. I went back to safe thoughts of childhood. But even they double-crossed me, because I had the terrible insight that my parents had come to care more for me than for each other. This kind of attention is what you dream about as a kid and run from as an adult.

I organized myself to the point of semisensibleness. Since *I* couldn't give him a divorce, the question occurred to me: What does Mother say about all this? Getting the upper hand over the ball in my throat, I inquired of Father, "What does Mother say about all this?"

That was another complication, he said, twiddling his watch chain. He hadn't told her anything. Now the ball was in charge. I could say nothing. Furth had to carry on. Mother had not been asked for a divorce, Mother had not been told about Elizabeth. Mother was, as they say, in the dark. I was stunned by his lack of decency toward his partner of thirty-five years, and I was shaken. Actually, I felt like the S word.

Chapter 30

Father and I spoke the next day. He told me he was going to tell Mother everything within the week. He didn't. A trip or something interfered. We spoke again. This time he vowed he would carry out his sad mission before the month was out. He didn't. I started to obsess about the situation, as though the burden were mine. He kept promising he would talk with Mother but somehow never did.

Then he asked if I would mind if he brought Elizabeth to a meeting in New Orleans where Furth and I would also be. *Mind?* I told him it was so far out of line that if he did I would never speak to him again. His position, as of the moment, I reminded him, was that of a guy who was keeping a dame, not someone with a divorce in the works. Since he was having such difficulty asking for his freedom, I suggested maybe he didn't really want it. No, no, he told me, he would speak to Mother within the week.

It was an odd quirk of fate that during this time a close woman friend of mine called, deeply troubled and torn. With great hesitation she confided that while she was in Spain with her husband, Father asked them to join him and Elizabeth for dinner. They declined. Elizabeth was apparently not the secret I had imagined, and Father's judgement was now seriously open to question.

I told him—between his trips in and out of Chicago—that his behavior had all the style of an alleycat and I was not going to stand by and watch him humiliate my mother. She, of all people, did not believe in "arrangements," and his conduct made it seem as though she either condoned this affair, or worse, was being played openly for a fool. Since he had informed me he was going to ask for a divorce, I suggested he do it . . .and if not, he should stash his lady friend and I would never say a word.

I finally did something startling even to myself. I gave Father a deadline. I told him if he didn't tell Mother within one more month's time, I would.

Thirty days from the time of my announcement, Father phoned from out of town. He was coming home and wanted me to know he would do what had to be done. When he arrived, he somehow never found the opportunity. A few days later he left Chicago. It was on that day I went to Mother's apartment. For four months I had shared Father's lousy secret . . .and for four months he had been promising to make a clean breast of things. I did not ask to know this family-shattering information and to be put in the middle; he had told me—he had put me there. If he wanted to mañana me. that was up to him, but I would do what I said I would do. If I no longer had any respect for my father, I would at least not lose respect for myself.

It is sticky business telling your mother that her husband wants a divorce but can't seem to bring it up. I decided I would not say much but I would say something.

It was an odd, if not surreal, encounter. We sat down in Mother's orange office adjoining their big bedroom. I seemed agitated, she noted. Well, a little, I said. What was wrong? she wanted to know.

"I think you should check on the state of your marriage."

"What are you talking about?" Mother asked, genuinely puzzled.

"That's all I'm going to say," I told her, and that is all I said. It killed me to come with that kind of cryptic message, but it would at least start them talking . . . because I knew she would ask him.

When Father returned from wherever he was, Mother repeated my remark. With great bravery, he denied knowing what I was talking about. The next day, when she asked him again, he told her everything. Now things were out in the open—which is a perfect place to get shot at.

It seems that in Father's confession of his wish for a divorce and a new wife he also told Mother I was only interested in his money and was mad at him because things were going poorly. He mentioned, also, that I was no friend of hers and had been bad-mouthing her for months.

I had no idea where his venom had come from, along with his rather odd view of reality. All I knew was he had turned on me and tried to leave Mother's and my relationship in ruins. I would spend months trying to make sense of all this.

Mother, in the meantime, was a marvel of strength and

acceptance. I don't think she had three bad days, total, after Father broke the news. She behaved just as she would have told others to behave: "Kwitcher bellyachin' buttercup," is how she often put it in the column. Though "shock" was the word Mother used to describe her response to Father's announcement, there must have been a secret alcove of her mind which was not surprised. The laws of emotional physics will not tolerate male menopause, alcohol, reverses,and depression without some explosive adjustment. The adjustment Father made was to leave his wife.

Symbolically, Elizabeth's profssion was an interesting one. She was a nurse, a caretaker . . .and Father didn't seem well.

The thought had dawned on him, too One night during dinner, before Mother knew anything he asked if she thought he ought to see a shrink. She said it was up to him. He asked her to make an appointment, since she knew the best in town. Mother said no, she wouldn't do that because she didn't want to *send* him to a psychiatrist, and besides, he knew the same ones she did. The next day he made his own appointmentand returned with the verdict: he had been to the doctor, and once was enough. He was sure there were no answers for him there.

He also gave AA a try. He went to several meetings and very much liked the people. He did not, however, stop drinking and eventually gave up the meetings because he said he traveled so much. Mother thought it would be indelicate to remind him that AA had chapters all over the world.

He was still knee-deep in business deals, however, and those that were pending caused him to ask a favor: could stay in the apartment? He was afraid his moving out might damage the deals. Mother thought about it, then gave him an answer. Sure, she said. Stay. Things hadn't been good for many months, so what was the difference? They both traveled and they would manage somehow. And so, from January 1975, Father lived at home as kind of a guest.

For my birthday, in March, Mother sent me a studio card with a frazzled-looking hippie on the front. "Think of what it means to be a member of our family," it said. "Then try to have a happy birthday anyway!" It was then that I really understood the situation. My parents were being divorced. I came from a broken home. I was thirty-five.

Father felt able to leave in mid-May, and when Mother returned from a speaking engagement in Greece, he was gone. When he moved out, the process of parting began. The end was no different from the middle or the beginning: Mother was still taking care of things.

She sent him dozens of new socks, shirts, shorts, and ties, along with two hats—"One to wear and one to lose." She had always bought his clothes and worried how he would look. She also sent over canned goods, lots of soup, and Ornade for when he got a cold.

Was this how she showed anger? I wondered. Well, that's not what she felt, she said. Why not? I asked. It was worth getting angry about. For whatever reason, Mother wouldn't—or couldn't—allow anger. I always thought it cleared the air; she thought it muddied the waters. What she did acknowledge, however, was worry. How would Father manage, and would he be all right? She instructed the lawyers to move quickly. That way, Father would be free to remarry. Then he wouldn't be alone.

I was astonished by Mother's generous behavior. Actually, I viewed her as some kind of sainted nut. All the divorces I knew about involved lengthy legal hassles and "losing" the gentleman's camera equipment—not sending over canned peaches and facilitating a remarriage. I finally decided that maybe you had to be fifty-seven to take the high road . . .or maybe you just had to be Eppie.

What saved her, perhaps, from feeling resentful and used-up was a gut feeling that the failure was not hers but one of luck. She had always said that "Life is what happens to you when you're making other plans." Now she would make new plans—alone—independent of the mate who had been part of everything for thirty-six years.

"When comes an hour of sadness, the need is there to talk." The first person Mother called was Ted Hesburgh. He said they would get together the next day. "It doesn't have to be tomorrow, "she said. "Yes it does," he answered, "either at Chicago or Notre Dame." Mother flew to South Bend the following morning and they talked for five hours—with Father Ted pretending had nothing else to do.

Bob Stolar, of course, was the rock he had always been. Having known Eppie and Jules better—and longer—than their other friends, he brought to the situation his knowledge of them both then and now.

Mother's East Coast chums insisted she come spend time with them. She called it being "america's house guest," with Art and Ann Buchwald, Walter and Betsy Cronkite, and Barbara Walters.

Popo was the first of the sisters to learn the news. The twins had patched things up and had, in fact, been warm and good friends for the last ten years. It was a more controlled friendship than before—they agreed not to talk about their work—but it was close and affectionate.

Popo wanted to come to Chicago, and she came, bringing with her a loving supportiveness that spoke of childhood comfort. It was not really a surprise that Popo was wonderful, but she was mercurial—and therefore unpredictable.

And then, of course, Mother's friend Mary Lasker did the perfect thing. She called to say she was having "something very special" at her place in upstate New York and Mother would be expected from June 30th through July, 4. The dates bridged Mother's anniversary and birthday, the second and fourth of July for Mary knew of past celebrations when Eppie, Jules, Popo, and Mort would all go on a birthday-anny-trip to places like Nairobi, Zagreb, Buenos Aires, Vienna. Now Mother would go to Mary's. Her dear "girlfriend" would fill in that time with a birthday party full of people Mother liked.

A lot of people knew my folks were finished, but the *people* didn't know. How should she announce her divorce? Mother wondered. What should be the form? We talked about the options. The Rockefellers, a while before, had announced it through a lawyer. Mother liked the simplicity of that. Nelson Rockefeller, however, did not write an advice column and Mother realized the lawyer approach would not work. Word had to come from her . . . and then she knew. If an estimated 65 million people daily read Ann Landers, she would tell them, through the column, in a statement of her own. This would be the third time a personal message had run in her space.

When she had worked through several drafts, she called and asked if I could come. It was a little before dinner. We

plunked down in the orange office and she handed me three
pages of yellow copy paper. I read her special column,
although it took a lot of time. Like Richard III, I
apologized, "Mine eyes are full of tears, I cannot see." It
was the most moving piece I had ever read, and of course
the more so because these people were my parents.

In my twenty years as Ann Landers this is the most
difficult column I have ever tried to put together.

I do so after many hours of soul-searching. Should
it be written at all? Would it be appropriate? Would
it be fair? I have decided yes—because you, my
readers, are also my friends. I owe it to you to say
something. There should be word directly from me.

The sad, incredible fact is that after thirty-six
years of marriage Jules and I are being divorced. As I
write these words, it is as if I am referring to a letter
from a reader. It seems unreal that I am writing
about my own marriage.

Many of you may remember the column that
appeared in 1969. It was in honor of our thirtieth
wedding anniversary. You may also recall the
column I wrote when my beloved mother-in-law,
Gustie Lederer, passed away. On both occasions I
gave you some intimate glimpses of our life
together. Thousands of readers were kind enough to
write and say they considered those columns my
best.

Every word that appeared in those columns was
true when I wrote them, and very little that was said
then could not be said today—is complete honesty.

Jules is an extraordinary man. His nickname for

me was "The Queen." He was loving, supportive, and generous. He is still all those things—and I will always cherish our wonderful years together.

That we are going our separate ways is one of life's strangest ironies. How did it happen that something so good for so long didn't last forever? The lady with all the answers does not know the answer to this one.

Perhaps there is a lesson there for all of us. At least it is there for me. Never say, "It couldn't happen to us!"

Please, don't write or call and ask for details. The response would be, "Sorry, this is a personal matter. . . . Time will not alter my position. I shall continue to say, No comment." There will be no compromising . . . no exceptions. Just wish us both well.

Not only has this been the most difficult column I have ever written, but also it is the shortest. I apologize to my editors for not giving you your money's worth today. I ask that you not fill this space with other letters. Please leave it blank—as a memorial to one of the world's best marriages that didn't make it to the finish line.

It ran on July 1, 1975, one day shy of their thirty-sixth anniversary.

One night Father called Furth about a real-estate matter and made one crack too many about my relationship to his money. When I was told the remark, I phoned Father to say that since he didn't think very well of me, it was my wish that we not be in touch at all. It was too painful to absorb his animosity, so why go through the charade of angry conversations disguised as civilized chat?

It looked, of course, as though I had rung off from Father because he left Mother. It was nothing I cared to set people straight about . . . and I wouldn't have known how to explain that my father blamed me for ending his marriage.

Actualy, he blamed a lot of people for a number of things. This one was an SOB, that one was a bastard; what's-his-name had double-crossed him and so-and-so had robbed him blind. This once sweet, open, giving guy was now transformed into a suspicious and embittered middle-aged man. This was not the father I had known . . . this was someone else.

I worked for weeks to understand how everything had changed, and why. A psychiatrist I trusted, Arthur Norton, gave me his ideas and helped me formulate my own. The key to everything, of course, was Father. He *was* his fortune in his head. When his wealth was diminished, so was he; if he was worth less, then he was worthless. His feelings about money were projected onto me. For all my big-spender adolescence, my attachment was not to his affluence but to his warmth.

The money thing was further twisted up because of Mother. Her success, reflected off his self-perceived failure, blinded him to the history between them . . . to the three and a half decades of sharing their lives. It was a close call as to whether he needed to split and run to block out her success or whether he wanted to end the relationship to spare her his reverses. If the drama in Father's thoughts was based on these two possibilities, clear thinking did not have a speaking part.

The machinations of Father coming to me, before

Mother, became clearer. He was conflicted about making the move at all. He really wanted to tell her, and then was mad because I did. I suspect that from his troubled perspective he wanted them both—Mother and Elizabeth—but knew that this was not to be. It would have been comforting to continue the relationship he had started building as a young man . . . with all the shared experiences, the child, the history; it would also have been nice to have the worshipful, younger, new woman, whom he could mold. The final decision seemed to be that Mother had her life and he needed a new one.

I worked through my feelings of guilt. I had, after all, given Mother some information; had I not, maybe they would be together. The doctor suggested there were other responses Mother might have had, such as "Mind your own business." or "Thank you for your concern, but there is nothing I wish to do about this." I had not created the trouble, it was pointed out. I had merely talked about it.

It was all over except the paperwork. Mother and Father had survived. Theirs was a cockeyed love stroy but one with rich memories; and a couple of lessons. My dear Adam, then ten, told me in the kitchen one day, "Well, now you know how it feels." I did, indeed, although my own three children, being young when thier father and I parted, probably had it tougher.

The divorce was granted October 17, 1975. It was heard in chambers by Hy Feldman, the father of one of my closest friends. I accompanied Mother to formally fulfill the function of a witness. Judge Feldman was thoughtful and discreet. In less than fifteen minutes the plaintiff was legally on her own.

It seems that Mother had worried more than I knew about Father being alone. She had extracted a pledge from him that he would remarry as soon as it was possible. He kept his promise and was married a week after the divorce was final . . . in London.

Chapter 31

While things were getting sorted out, Mother had been on automatic pilot. She canceled speaking dates here and there, did no radio or TV, and wrote the column from some remembered sense of industry. But now she could return to work with total application. She immersed herself in her career — a little as a therapeutic pool but mostly because the waters were familiar, and she liked them. With the "girls" in the office urging her on, Mother went back to a full speaking calendar. Byron knew it all along: "The busy have no time for tears."

"The mouth circuit," as Mother called it let her feel the pulse and press the flesh. She spoke about her work and what she'd learned. She didn't give The Speech, as some celebrities did, because her audiences were too diverse. One part that never changed, however, was something of a trademark: her acknowledgment of the group that asked her. If it was, to say, doctors in Sheboygan, she would take this tack: "I could talk to you tonight about medicine. Or I could talk about Sheboygan. I could even talk about sex. Maybe I'll just talk about the sex lives of the doctors in Sheboygan."

Feedback from the speeches was crucial to the column. What Ann Landers heard around the country allowed her viewpoint to change with the times. I do not consider Mother to be in the forefront of social experimentation, but neither does she believe anymore that a twenty-year-old person needs to be a virgin.

From wanderlust or fervency it was Mother's pleasure to fly from Kalamazoo to Cleveland, then to Poughkeepsie and Port Washington. She liked the parties and the people and the act of holding forth. One of the secretaries usually went along. (Probably to make sure she didn't misread the flight number for the departure time.)

Mother has remarked that the thing which makes her feel oldest is, when she flies, one stewardess — or two — telling her they remember when she spoke at their high schools. Such speeches, by the way, are now infrequent. There is no longer the need, Mother feels, to speak to high school audiences because information is more readily available now. In the 1950's and early 1960's, however, she was almost alone in talking about premarital sex and VD.

Her divorce, ironically, added a dimension to her work. Whereas Father worried it would detract from her credibility, it seems to have made her more human. People identify with trouble, and now they knew she'd had some, too. Mother's observation in her speeches was apparently correct: "Trouble is the great equalizer."

My children thought the breakup of Grandma's marriage

had a positive side effect. "It mellowed her out," they decided. She agreed that, yes, perhaps, the kids were right. In fact, Mother and I had a joke between us: A funny thing happened to her on her way to sainthood. She got divorced.

The scar tissue between Father and me was hardening, not healing. The longer we didn't speak, the easier it got . . . but I had terrible feelings of regret. Where was that terrific man I had loved, and why had he not stayed the same? I didn't care that he'd made a new life, but I couldn't understand why the old one was in pieces at his feet. Not only had he withdrawn from Mother and me and many old chums, but also he had written off Morton, his oldest and best friend. Nobody's behavior suited him; the world had done him wrong.

Father began to seem tragic, in my mind, and became a figure of torment. He was Willy Loman . . . or maybe King Lear. It was all evened up, however, because I knew he saw me as Goneril or Regan.

I bumped into him only once. It was in a bookstore. He was paying for something at the counter. When I saw him, I was already in the store. There was no choice but to speak. We exchanged formal hellos and he asked after the children. He hadn't seen them in months and blamed me, assuming if they didn't want to see him that I had told them not to. It was hardly that simple, of course. The real reason was that kids have responsive antennae and they instinctively figured if their mother and grandfather weren't speaking that they'd better stay away.

I must have wanted a thaw in the situation, because I asked, impulsively, if he wanted to go for a cup of coffee. "No," he said, "I'm too busy," and out the door he went. I give up, I thought. There is no way back from this one.

I saw him one more time from a distance. I was riding an escalator down in the Hancock Building, where he had his offices. He was riding up. I looked across at him, this sad familiar father, and felt faint. I held the moving rail tightly in order not to fall. I knew then that we would never fix it up. Stubbornness was part of me . . . and I got mine from him.

It was an odd bit of timing that in 1976, when the dust had settled from my parents' divorce, another marriage in our family came apart. Mine. Jules Furth and I weren't going to make it. It was sad rather than rancorous, and we agreed to go our separate ways. We'd been together four and a half years.

Abra and Cricket were comfortable with the situation. No one had gotten particularly close to Furth. Adam, however, when I told him, made a face that said: Oh my God.

"Adam," I asked, "were you attached to Jules?"

"No," he said, "but my friends will think you're crazy."

His friends and my mother, I thought. It occurred to me that a twice-divorced daughter seemed rather peculiar—especially for her. I was so concerned, in fact, about what she would think that I dilly-dallied for days before telling her. And when I did, I made a disclaimer meant to give her confidence. "I will not marry again," I said.

She was not shook-up, as I had imagined, and she didn't think that I was nuts. She did, however, suggest that I had been looking for the wrong things. "It's those lousy movie magazines," she said, "and the popular press in general. Young people today have no idea what to expect. Do not delude yourself," she warned, "that you will meet a movie star and life will be wonderful."

I met the movie star December 3, 1976. I interviewed him for the Chicago *Daily News*. I had returned to work when Furth and I separated. One of the executives observed that writing seemed to be what Margo did between husbands.

Ken Howard opened in the play *Equus* on a Thursday. Our interview was set for Friday. The arrangements were that I would pick him up at NBC, where he was taping *Kup's Show*. I didn't pay much attention to that segment, visiting, instead, with Twiggy's manager and Tom Wolfe. When the taping was over, I introduced myself to Howard. It was not an auspicious beginning. As we walked the corridors of NBC, he looked down at me — and I mean down, because he is six-foot-six — and said, "How ya' doin'?" Oh, good, I thought. A dumb ballplayer.

The dumb ballplayer turned out to be the best man I ever met — an Amherst graduate who'd gone on to Yale Drama School, Broadway, movies, and TV. Our luncheon interview went on for four hours, followed by a two-hour cup of coffee and an after-theater snack that night. We just never could stop talking, and were married three and a half months later.

Mother was thrilled. She liked his fineness, his warmth, and his commitment to my children. "The Gorgeous Goy," as she called him, could even speak Yiddish . . . well, maybe not *speak* but he knew a lot of words. Mother decided she'd been wrong all these years about interfaith marriages, and subsequently made it a point, on television and in her column, to say she no longer believed that religious differences mattered. Find the right person, she said, and pray however you want.

There were people, of course, who couldn't resist giving Mother the needle. "Oh, her *third* marriage," they would say. "How *nice.*" She was, in fact, surprisingly cool about my three husbands. She did wonderfully, I thought, at a dinner in New York. A young man stopped by her table and said, "I went to school with your son-in-law." She didn't want to say, "Which one?" so she said, "Where?" When the answer was Amherst, she knew how to proceed.

If my mother was thrilled, my children were ecstatic. Here was this guy who would talk to them for hours—and not only talk, but listen. There were other pluses, as well. Cricket got an in-house gymnastics coach and Adam had a B-ball chum. Abra needed "one more pet," so Ken came through with "Rabbit Redford."

Adam, not yet eleven, offered a challenge one night. "Now that you've married us," he asked, "when ya gonna settle down and go into business?"

Chapter 32

W e moved to California, where Ken thought he should be. With Adam's question much on his mind, he made a lunch date with a friend, Bruce Paltrow.

"I have an idea for a series," he said. "Wanna be the producer?"

"Sure," said Paltrow, "but why do you want to do another series?"

"Oh," Ken smiled, "so I can settle down and go into business."

Ken's idea was to base a series on his high-school basketball career. He would play the coach. The Messers Howard and Paltrow declared themselves partners and made an appointment to talk to the brass at CBS. They sold the show and called it *The White Shadow*. With the impetus from Adam and the energy from Bruce, Ken had found a way to settle down—at least for a while—and go into business.

Two years later, in the summer of 1979, someone I knew moved to Los Angeles. My father. When Mother told me his address, I thought, "My God, we're neighbors." He and Elizabeth lived three miles away. I worried about bumping into them . . . then I just worried about bumping into him. Never having met Elizabeth, I wouldn't know who I was bumping into.

I told the children that Grandpa lived nearby. Adam thought he'd like to get in touch. He made the call and reached Elizabeth. Father was in Texas but would return the call the following afternoon.

Adam was never home during the day, however. He was "working" on the *White Shadow* set. When Father called, I was totally unprepared to hear his voice. It had been four years since our conversation in the bookstore.

"Is Adam there?" he said.

"No I'm sorry, he's at work."

"What does he do?"

"He's a gopher."

"What is a gopher?"

"Go fer coffee, go fer hamburgers."

"Well, tell him his grandfather called."

"Do you know who this is?" I asked.

"I believe I remember the voice."

I then invited him, at Adam's request, to come visit us the following Saturday at three o'clock.

When he arrived, I greeted him alone. He was a little heavier and a lot grayer. He looked older, I thought, but he

238

was still Father, down to the FDR cigarette holder.

The meeting wasn't particularly comfortable and it certainly wasn't warm. Too much time had elapsed for the children to relate as they once had, and the strain between Father and me was apparent. But at least we were speaking—although not a whole lot. I busied myself inside while everyone else stayed on the patio. It was important that I be in the kitchen, making coffee and squeezing orange juice, drinking ice water and hiding. The outside group was Ken, Father, and the children. Then it was just Ken and Father, the children straying off to spare themselves the awkwardness of the occasion.

Ken told me later their talk had been open and warm; that Father seemed involved in making a new start, was on something of a health kick, and had a new business venture in mind. They had never met before . . . the husband and the father.

"I like him," Ken declared. "You should try to see him as he is."

"I can't," I shrugged. "I want to see him as he was."

Ken, the kids, and I had grown to be a family. Father was a "neighbor," and Mother was content. It was 1980 and her business had been going for a quarter of a century. Ann Landers, Eppie-style, was twenty-five years old. Referred to as the most widely syndicated column in the world, it claimed a readership of 70 million people in more than 1,000 papers. The work was certainly tailor-made for the personality. What better outlet than an advice column for a woman who was teacher, preacher, Florence Nightingale, and Joan of Arc?

All the things Mother cared about were handled in the column. Advice to the lovelorn was now for the lifeworn. Se had taken the form and made it her own. Any question was fair game, and anyone could ask it. For the price of a stamp the human condition seemed manageable. Mother turned into America's umpire.

Her style was derivative, the approach was her own. An aggregate of phrases and collected opinions helped her sell a value system. Ann Landers was experts . . . Ann Landers was Eppie. One pop analyst declared her writings more closely akin to Aristotle's *Ethics* than any other contemporary writer's. Not bad for a college dropout from Iowa.

She was a paradox, of course. The ultimate liberated woman, she played the game—the old-fashioned one—in which she never acknowledged the degree to which her life was her own. It seemed funny and fey that "Jules' wife" was sewn into the linings of her furs all te years they were married. It was a remark, however, that she didn't wish to be regarded as off on her own. It was nothing she cared to think about . . . just smething she wanted to do.

Mother's life and work were intertwined about a hundred times more than most people's. Her interests, perforce, wove the two together. It was not possible for her to leave Ann Landers at home. People were too interested in what "she" had to say. The dual identity, Eppie/Ann, was fate's compensation. If she was "half an egg," according to her mother, she was also two people. The numbers worked out in the end.

It is legitimate to compare two writers in the same field, and inrresistible when they are twins. With time, it mattered less to Mother that Popo had made it a sister act.

Comparisons turned out to be compliments; many professionals judged Ann Landers the more substantial and less comedic. Reader surveys said so, too.

It had to feel good to outdistance Popo in the commendation sweepstakes, but the real gift of the column was that it gave Mother a focus. Her work was what she valued, the commitment absolute. She'd learned from years of letters the terrible burdens people carried. It would have been hard for her to go to pieces over her own problems. She knew too much to imagine that a sister who horned in—or even a husband who had left—was a major tragedy. She had other things to do besides lick her wounds. There were letters to answer and places to be. The column was now her center, and she and it served each other well.

The aura of advice followed Mother like perfume. People offered up their problems, then did just as she advised. Political friends, however, did things a little differently. They asked for her opinion and did precisely something else.

Robert Kennedy, when he was deciding whether or not to run for president, asked to see Mother while he was in Chicago. What did she think, he asked, about his chances? "It's not your turn," she said.

Hubert Humphrey asked the same question more than once . . . and every time the answer was, "Don't run." Mother pleaded with him, particularly, not to be Lyndon Johnson's running mate. This may have been a split decision: he ran and won . . . but regretted it. Three weeks after the inauguration, Winston Churchill died. Johnson had the flu and couldn't fly to England. With a long tradition of vice-presidents filling in in such situations, Hubert had one foot out the door. The president sent Earl Warren, then the Chief Justice.

"What do you think about who's going to the Churchill funeral?" Hubert asked on the phone. "It's just to let you know where you stand," Mother told him.

In 1976 the peanut farmer was Mother's choice. He never ignored her advice—but neither did he ask for any. Although Ann Landers did not endorse candidates, she wanted to help. She helped. When Carter, the hopeful, flew into Chicago, Old Ep was there to meet him . . . and incidentally to make the nightly news. My eyes fell out of my head when I saw them on television. Mother and Carter were hugging hello.

Question: "Miss Landers, are you endorsing Jimmy Carter?"

Answer: "Oh, no, I never endorse anyone. I've just come to greet a friend."

Greet a friend, indeed. I called her at home. Surely she had better things to do than stumping for the wimp, I said. I could not believe she had done this. "He's a great guy," she said. "You'll see. He'll do amazing things."

She was not altogether wrong. One amazing thing the great guy did was motivate her to vote Republican four years later. Mother had been wrong about Carter, and said so.

Her value to Democratic politicians was multifaceted. She had veteran's credentials, having been a party official and an insider for years. Her already canny instincts had been sharpened by the column. To put it in Chicagoese, she

242

put it in Chicagoese, she had "clout." Appropriately enough, it was never more apparent than at Mayor Daley's funeral.

The rites, of course, were private and by invitation only. Dignitaries were flying in from everywhere. Boston's mayor, Kevin White, called Mother the day before the funeral. Would she like to ride with him? She'd love to, she said.

When Kevin's car came by for her at nine the next morning, there was no mistaking the event. Mother was dressed all in black, including a veil and a black fur coat. "Jeez," said Kevin, "you look like the widow."

"But do I look like I have a ticket?" She laughed.

"You're kidding, Eppie. You don't hve a ticket? How are you going to get in?"

"I'll take my chances," She shrugged.

Within twenty minutes they were in a long line of slowly moving cars. As they approached the Nativity of Our Lord's Church, they had to stop for a barricade. A cop walked over to the car. Looking in side, the officer did not say anything about tickets and ID. What he said was "Hi, Annie. Who's your friend?"

A block from the church they were stopped at a second barricade. Kevin was getting ready to identify himself when a security man spotted Mother. "You gotta be Ann Landers," he said. "You helped me raise my kids." There was no mention of showing ID, and he waved them on.

In front of the cathedral was a cluster of Secret Service men and dozens of local police. Mother and Kevin got out of the car and started to walk inside. They were stopped by a plainclothesman. He started to ask for tickets but was interrupted by Earl Bush, Mayor Daley's press secretary. "I'll take over," he said, and did. Then he whispered to Mother, "I don't see your name on the chart, Ann, but I know you're with the VIP's." He seated them in the third row, behind Ted Kennedy, Nelson Rockefeller and Fritz Mondale. They, in turn, were behind President Carter, Governor-elect Jim Thompson, and Sarge Shriver.

The mayor of Boston shook his head in disbelief. "This is amazing," he said.

Mother handed him a Bible. "Stick with me, dear, and someday you might amount to something."

In September 1981 Mother was up to her old tricks. She was still stirring the pot with her advice. The only difference this time was that no one had asked her a thing. It was just one of those opportunities that was too good to pass up.

She was at the White House dinner for Menahem Begin and was apparently overcome with all those decision-makers in one room. She took her best shot and approached the man she'd known the longest: Caspar Weinberger, Secretary of Defense. "Look, Cap," she said, "you've got to dump the MX missile. It's a dog. By the time it's completed, it'll be obsolete."

If that was not what the secretary was expecting to hear at a state dinner—especially from Mother—she went on to give him some ideas about where to put the money he'd save from dumping his missile, the dog. School-lunch programs, child care, national institutes of mental health, Head Start, and aid to the handicapped.

She wasn't holding her breath waiting for the announcement that the MX was dead. But she had to "suggest" it anyway, you see, because she believed it to be right.

Chapter 33

Schopenhauer chose porcupines to symbolize ambivalence. The creatures needed to get close for warmth, but nearness made for pain. The prick of a quill would move them apart, but then they'd get cold and inch closer again. Hurting each other was always a risk, but being together was worth it.

Mother and Popo were porcupines. Their lives were all about intervals—coming together and moving apart. And they'd had good luck—for seventeen years—with not hurting each other too badly. From 1964, when they patched things up, to 1981, there'd been only an occasional slip. They would jab at each other once in a while, but mostly there were good times and they kept each other warm. Then all of a sudden the cycle was ended when dozens of quills were dipped, appropriately enough, in ink. Popo gave an interview in *The Ladies' Home Journal* to a fellow named Cliff Jahr. It was an extraordinary piece to read. Popo claimed she had ghosted the early Ann Landers that Mother was the envious overshadowed sister, an also-ran with lousy luck. Popo felt compelled to talk about how old Mother looked, and her careless disregard for Father.

Forget that it sounded delusional, who talks about that kind of stuff? And why? The writer mentioned that part of the interview took place "while dining with wine and candlelight." Perhaps there was too much candlelight. Johr wrote that Dear Abby spoke of her own good luck—"I've led a charmed life"—but repeated herself three and four times with "a clenched hand slapping the table." She seemed like a woman screaming at the neighbors about how wonderful her life was.

Why had this shabby performance been given? There were several possibilities, and readers thought of them all. Mother's office was deluged with mail. People suggested Popo may not have been sober, or perhaps was in need of professional help. It struck many that the envy she assigned to Mother was really her own.

And Popo was talking too much about money. She seemed to need to validate the fact that she was rich.

> Our values are a little bit different. She was going to marry for money and I was going to marry for love. Well, I married for both and she married a heck of a nice guy, but he didn't have a quarter. In Eau Claire she had a tiny little place, while I lived in a lovely home with loads of help. Her husband worked for mine. I drove a luxury car; she drove a lower-priced model. And that had to hurt. Look, she needs a lot of reinforcement.

. . . She suffered a heck of a lot. If she looked old, if she needed a face lift, believe me, it's because she needed it. I'm quite opposed to chopping myself up, but it was her right. Why not? When you cry a lot, it's got to show.

Maybe Popo had amnesia. Inasmuch as she'd had her own eyes done, and her thighs, the chopping remark was quite peculiar. But more to the point, it didn't behoove a human-relations counselor to dish her sister. Popo had not covered herself with glory on this one.

It was actually rather fascinating, though, . . . like watching a trailer roll over a cliff. In the midst of all the meanness, Popo spoke of loyalty and love: "We are each other's best friend. I'd fight like a tiger for my sister and she'd do the same for me."

It was an odd, jarring piece. Popo was working hard to make Mother look bad, yet declaring how happy her own life had been: "'I haven't missed a thing,' she said. 'Plee-e-ease, if I go tomorrow—' she breaks off, smiles enigmatically, and clinks glasses, 'nobody cry for me.'"

The finale to the *Journal* saga was interesting. Popo made her petty statements, many of which weren't true, then denied having said them. The denial became fainter, however, because Mr. Jahr had her on tape and made it plain he didn't wish to hear, one more time, that he made up all the quotes. Her explanation then became one of ill will: the writer took the very worst of what she said in order to make her look bad.

Mother's reaction was not to respond. What was there to say, after all, about an article so astoundingly hostile that the wire services picked up the "highlights" and newspapers wrote about its unkindness? Mother passed up the chance to lash back, I believe, so as not to sully her work. And that was the difference between them. Mother's career was a calling. She wanted it to have stature and dignity, and you couldn't have that and call people names, too.

An unlikely third party proposed a rebuttal; Father called Mother in an absolute rage. He was going to talk to some papers about how "charmed" Popo's life really was and refute her interview point by point. Mother convinced him he must not talk to any press people about anything he knew. He finally agreed, if that was her wish. "I've always been in your corner, doll," he said. I liked him for that, for the first time in years.

And I thought about the porcupines—my mother and my aunt. The quills were there and always would be, but the twinship pull was stronger. A solution seemed unlikely at the age of sixty-three. The Zen admonition was probably true: There is no solution . . . seek it lovingly.

The through line of my mother's life for years has been her work. It has mattered, it has counted, and it sustains her even now. I never thought about how long she'd been Ann Landers until I heard a speech she gave in 1981. It was the commencement address for Adam's class at Eaglebrook. He was the same age then as I had been when Mother began the column. Her work had touched three generations of our family.

Adam, of course, was mortified that his grandmother was the speaker. Ninth-graders bound for prep school didn't need a speech from her. Why not "Magic" Johnson . . . or maybe Bobby Orr?

Addressing her marks to the graduates, Mother introduced herself. "You may not believe this, but once I was fifteen years old." Then she went on to proffer some advice: mind your own business, decide what you want to be in life and work toward that goal, don't be afraid to fail, and be honorable in your dealings. Then she made her pitch—as she did with older audiences—only this time it was in the idiom of young people:

Now, I am not telling you how to live your life. Everyone has the right to choose his own ways. But my decision—no cigarettes, no booze, and no drugs—was a good one for me. And I believe it helped me to stay well and energetic and do the things in life that I wanted to do. Besides that, I don't think I look too bad for an old girl who's been around since World War I.

So I say to you, take care of your head as well as your body. The two are very closely related. Hate, hostility, jealousy, bitterness, and self-pity are poisons. Don't let them get into your system. . . . Now, I am not going to stand up here and tell you to love everybody; in the first place, everybody doesn't deserve it. I am sure you are going to meet people out there who are two-faced, weird, obnoxious, dishonest, and have crummy values. So I say to you, steer clear of those characters. But hate, no, it is a terrible waste of energy.

And finally, expect trouble in your life, because it will catch up with you sooner or later. Nobody escapes it. Trouble does not mean you are stupid or bad or guilty of some wrongdoing; it simply means you are a member of the human race. Remember it is not what happens to you that counts, but how you handle it. . . . You will discover as you get older that life isn't always fair. Whatever it is that hits the fan is never evenly distributed; some people always manage to get more than others.

When she wrapped it up, there was a marvelous ovation. Even Adam said it was "pretty good" and that all his friends had liked it. One chum, however, told him that he never realized Ann Landers had such a Midwestern accent. "She seems to put," he said, "an R in every word."

One of the things she told the boys was a rather earthy phrase: "No one ever drowned in his own sweat." It was corny, obvious, old, and true, but Mother believed it and lived it herself. She had learned, long ago, that finding a task and zeroing in was a foolproof path to fulfillment.

Her message was Work! and her sermon was Do! Maybe she was born with the Russian work ethic that Chekhov talked about in *The Three Sisters,* where Tusenbach is constantly extolling work: it will fulfill us, he says, and bring us great joy.

Mother seemed jejune, at times, with her enthusiasms and her sense of mission. But she was an authentic doer with the quality of everyone from Andrew Jackson to Knute Rockne—that special something that got things done.

Just as interviewers ask hundred-year-old people their secrets for longevity, so Mother is asked the key to her productivity. Her one-line answer has become: "I don't drink, smoke, or get mixed up with bores." Since I do all three, her answer is a lovely reminder that I am a grown-up and that she has let me become one. I don't think a mother can do any more.

As for the other part of her life, there will never be another Ann Landers—in the literal sense. When the Field executives gave her the rights to the name, they knew the column would end with her. How long will she continue? As long as she lives. "They will find me one day," she has said, "with my last column in the typewriter." I believe that is the way it will happen.

New York—December 1981